Lemonade to Gold

A Gift For

From

Judy Risner

Turning Your Dreams into Reality

LEMONADE
to
GOLD

Judy Risner

Lemonade to Gold

Second Edition

Copyright © 2012 by Judy Risner. All rights reserved

No part of this publication may be reproduced, stored in a retrieval system or transmitted in any way by any means, electronic, mechanical, photocopy, recording or otherwise without the prior permission of the author except as provided by USA copyright law.

All recommendations are made without guarantee on the part of the author. The author and publisher disclaim any liability in connection with the use of this information.

Published in the United States of America

ISBN 978-0-9972952-0-7

Endorsements

"A great tool when feeling indecisive and lacking a road map to bring about change. Judy's book designs a plan for making dreams come true and going beyond what was thought possible."

Shelly Short, RDH, MS, PhD
Life Management Coach
Co-Creator Zum Wohl, LLC

"As an entrepreneur and executive coach, I have endorsed this type of methodology for years with great results. I was so happy to find that Judy's book offers a simple format for anyone to work with the three tools: problem solving, achieving goals, and making decisions. An extra bonus is that her book is filled with terrific pearls of wisdom and sage advice to create a positive environment for personal growth for everyone, no matter where you are on your journey."

Carole L. Lape BA, CEC
Principal and Executive Business Coach
Harrison James Group

"Lemonade to Gold offers every reader clear, simple, and effective ways to understand and incorporate the powerful tools of goal attainment, decision making, and problem solving. Whether your aim is to strategically plan for business success or enrich your personal life, Judy's insight, instruction, and words of wisdom will be a comfortable companion wherever you are on that journey."

Vicki C. Sanco, Principal
Journey Management Group, LLC
Consulting, Coaching, Training for the Dental Professional

Dedication

To Don, my husband and soul mate, for always supporting me while I follow my dreams.

To my children and grandchildren, may you always use God's gifts to reach your true potential, as you follow your dreams.

Acknowledgments

I would like to thank my dear friends and colleagues; Dr. Carl Schreiner and Dr. Terry Schreiner, for taking a chance on me over thirty years ago. Your continued faith in my ability and your ongoing support has helped me realize my true potential.

A special *thank you* to all my friends and colleagues for taking the time out of your busy lives to offer feedback and support during this project. Here's to us; as we help each other continue on our paths!

To my family, I'll always have a deep appreciation for the encouragement and support you have shown me during this project. Most of all, thank you for listening without judging. I love you all.

CONTENTS

- Goal Setting   9
- Steps of Goal Setting   13
- Problem Solving   31
- Steps of Problem Solving   33
- Decision Making   49
- Steps of Decision Making   51
- Life-Changing Results Shared by Others   61
- Choose to Feel Better   96
- Increase Happiness – Positive Thinking   121
- Get It in Writing   137
- Goal Setting Templates   138-157
- Problem Solving Templates   158-197
- Decision Making Templates   198-217
- Personal Notes   218-223
- About the Author   224
- Contact Information   226
- Contributors   229

GOAL SETTING

Many of us go through each day thinking and dreaming about the future. We dream about what we want to accomplish in our careers, as well as our personal lives. Some of us continue to dream about the possibilities, while others put a plan into place to turn their dreams into realities. Have you ever dreamed of accomplishing something that seemed out of reach? Did you quickly begin convincing yourself that there was *no way* to make it happen?

I believe there is a plan for all of us, and if we are open to guidance along the way we will eventually see our path clearly. My own life experiences have proven that hard work, perseverance, and following my passion all play key roles in helping me achieve my goals. I have also learned that praying for guidance from the very beginning to end, will lead me in directions I would never have imagined or planned. Knowing I'm on the right path has given me the courage and perseverance that remains crucial to help me stay the course.

I have always been a list writer and have found it helpful to make lists for everything from what needed to be picked up at the grocery store to what my next goals in life would be. When I decided to go to dental hygiene school I was a bit overwhelmed with how I could make it happen with two small children at home, in addition, to working a full time job. I began by making a list of steps I needed to take to be eligible to apply to the program. Then, as each step was completed, I would mark it off my list.

While in college, I began learning more about goal setting. You can compare goal setting to list making in some ways. The benefit of goal setting is that it helps you accomplish bigger, more complex goals or dreams by breaking them down into smaller tasks. It is a tool that you can use to help you focus on making your dreams come true one step at a time.

There are hundreds, possibly thousands, of books on the theory of goal setting. The goal-setting theory has been around for a long time and was first introduced by Aristotle and then in the late 1960s by Dr. Edwin Locke. This theory has withstood the test of time and has been proven to be a solid method to help you continue on the path you desire.

Making Your Dreams Come True

Writing your goals is a wonderful tool to use to get your dreams down on paper so you can make them become reality, otherwise they will remain only dreams. Sometimes the dream or goal can seem out of reach when you look at the big picture, and this method will help it seem less daunting. You will find that the goal-setting process will help you identify smaller, more attainable steps that will lead you toward accomplishing your overall goal. Following are some of the things I have learned along the way that have played a key role in making my dreams become a reality and have helped me focus on the direction I needed to take next.

- **Prioritize goals.** You may have more than one goal. It is important to prioritize your goals in the order of how you want to accomplish them. Put them in order of importance. What do you want to accomplish first?

- **Position yourself toward your goals.** Begin by thinking about what you want. Then begin heading in that direction by following the steps of goal setting. For example, if you want to climb Mt. Everest, you might want to start getting into shape...

- **Never share your goals with someone who won't support you.** You must remain committed to what you want to accomplish. Don't let others take you off your course.

- **Never give up.** Take it one day at a time and ask, "What do I need to do today to follow what is meant for me?" Be patient and continue moving forward, step by step, each and every day.

- **Follow your passion.** What would you like to be doing even if you didn't get paid for it? Listen to what your heart is telling you, and pray for guidance.

You can do this!

Follow These Steps of Goal Setting

1. Write your goal.

2. Write a detailed plan of how you are going to accomplish your goal. Write out the specific steps one by one.

3. Write beside each step the person who is going to be responsible for that step. (Your name may be by all steps.)

4. Assign a time/date deadline by each step. By what date are you going to have that step completed?

5. Re-evaluate. How is your plan working? Do you need to make any changes to the plan above? Re-write the plan as needed following the same steps listed above.

6. From beginning to end, pray for guidance. Are you on the right track for what is meant for you? I have found it is crucial to ask, "Is this the direction in which I need to be headed? If so, give me strength. If not, detour me in the right direction." Ask for the wisdom to know the difference. (This step is not necessarily included

in the steps of goal setting but has been instrumental in my own personal accomplishments.) This last step has truly made the difference in my personal growth. *Take it one step at a time. You will reach the goals that are meant for you!*

Leap of Faith

Later in this book I describe the decision-making process I went through when deciding whether or not I should stay with my current job or take a leap of faith and explore another direction. I ultimately made the decision to leave my corporate position, but quickly found myself wondering, *Now what?* Those who know me well would testify that not having a concrete plan is completely out of character for me. I tend to be that person who always has a detailed *plan A* outlined and options B and C waiting in the wings if plan A doesn't work out. Now I needed a new game plan and had no doubt that the next step would be to list my new goals and begin designing a plan.

I began my new journey by waking up each day; praying for guidance and began exploring my options. First, I made a list of how I wanted to spend my time and how I could replace my lost income. I brainstormed all the possibilities and included things I had been trained to do as well as things I always wanted to do but for which I had no prior training. The sky was the limit when making my list; if it crossed my mind as something worth exploring, it went on my list.

My list looked something like this:

Career Goals

- Continue to teach others basic skills to inspire them to reach for their goals.

- Continue working with dental teams to help them get their systems in place.

- Teach teambuilding and communication skills to help ensure teams look forward to going to work every day and enjoy their time together.

- Network with other consultants to continue to enhance my skills.

- Stay in touch with past colleagues for mutual support and learning experiences.

- Donate time to teach other groups basic skills.

- Continue improving and promoting my website to inspire users to never give up on their ideas and dreams.

- Revise and improve my book on goal setting and use as a teaching tool.

As I read my list, it was apparent that there was one common theme. My passion was teaching the basic principles I've outlined in the book and continue to inspire others to take charge of their lives and design the plan that's right for them. Through my consulting business, my website, and my book, this would all be possible.

My Plan

Next, I listed each of the three areas where I wanted to place my focus and began designing a plan under each goal.

Consulting

- Get the word out that I'm available to provide consulting independently.

Website

- Make it more, user-friendly.

- Get the word out to encourage others to share their stories

- Add more content.

- Seek professional website design.

Revise Book

- Add true stories that will help readers see how others applied the skills.

- Share more of my own experience.

- Seek professional help.

Then I looked at my topics and prioritized. I decided to spend a set amount of time each day on my website, book, and consulting career. Realizing my most immediate need was to replace my lost income, I chose to focus initially on my consulting career. I didn't really know where to start, but one thing was for sure: I knew if I put it in writing, it would help me bring some clarity to my options. Here's what it looked like:

Step 1: Identify goal:

- I want to continue consulting.

Step 2: Design the plan:

- Call friends and colleagues in the business and get the word out that I'm available.

- Visit with doctors in the area.

- Network through E-mail.

- Continue to go to dental meetings.

- Join professional groups for support.

Step 3: Determine the person responsible:

- My name by all steps

Step 4: Time activate by setting deadlines:

- Begin calling friends and colleagues <u>today</u> and discuss how we can support each other today. Set up <u>monthly</u> calls to continue support.

- Choose a nearby town and visit at least three doctors in each area each week <u>beginning Monday</u>.

- E-mail ten doctors by Friday of each week starting <u>next Friday</u>.

- Go online <u>tomorrow</u> and check out the next state and regional dental meetings and sign up to attend.

- Select which professional groups to join by the <u>end of the month</u>.

Step 5: Re-evaluate:

- Continue to visit with doctors in surrounding areas. I have been well received and it's been fun meeting a lot of great people.

- E-mails are not getting a great response. Continue to do on a limited basis, but follow up with a call.

- Continue going to dental meetings. Lots of great contacts made and saw many friends and had great fun!

- Joined two new professional groups,

which was a great decision. This has helped me network with others while providing another outlet for learning.

I'm excited to tell you what happened next! As I continued working on my goals, I began receiving calls from other professionals asking me to do some contract consulting. *Wow.* I was ecstatic and very honored that they would trust me with their clients. The first month I was unemployed, I received a call to work locally, and I couldn't have been more thrilled. I was able to do what I loved doing: help the client, help support the other consultant, *and* make some money. I felt very blessed and thanked God for the opportunity and continued with my plan. Then, out of the blue, the following month, a call came in for a request to help with another client, and then the next month; another client, and on and on until *every* month I received a call for help. I truly felt like this was part of the plan that was meant for me. Throughout my entire plan, I continued to pray for guidance to help me stay on the right path. I had complete faith that if I followed my instinct and worked hard, the money and support I needed would come.

Change Happens

A funny thing happened, early on, while working on my plan. It began to take another direction. It all started with requests for my business card, and I knew I needed something to leave with doctors so they could easily contact me. Well, to design a business card, I had to decide what to put on it. How should it read? What should it say? I also had been wondering how to handle the income I had been receiving since I was now, self-employed. A call to my accountant followed, and it quickly became apparent that I needed to establish a formal business to support my consulting work. Okay, now where do I start?

It seemed like such a daunting task, and I knew it would be important to break it down into smaller tasks. First, I began putting all my thoughts and questions down on paper. My list included things such as, what should I name the company; what kind of logo do I need to have; what kind of company it will need to be etc., LLC, corporation; do I need a tax ID number; when should I start marketing my company; how will I get the word out; how will I pay for everything I need to do; what should I do first?

Once I had my list completed, I began using the goal-setting principles to design my plan.

Step 1: Identify goal:

- Establish Consulting Business

Step 2: Design the plan:

- Brainstorm on what to name the company.

- Design a logo for company.

- Contact Oklahoma Small Business Development Center for basic information on how to start a business.

- Marketing plan—how do I get the word out?

Step 3: Determine the person responsible

- My name was by all steps. *Oh, the joy of being self-employed.*

Step 4: Time activate by setting deadlines

- Determine name of company in the next three days.

- Begin designing logo using computer graphics in the next three days after name of company is set. Complete by the 15th of the month.

- Contact Oklahoma Small Business Development center today.

- Hold on formal marketing plan until business basics have been established.

Step 5: Re-evaluate:

- Name has been set. It will be named Judy Risner Consulting, LLC.

- Hire a *professional* to design logo! I am at a roadblock and need help. What I'm doing is not working. Begin researching online for logo designers.

- Contact the Oklahoma Small Business Development Center for basic information on how to start a business was very helpful. Wow! What a great resource for anyone wanting to start a business. I was very impressed by the comprehensive nature of their website. I printed the "business basics" booklet and followed their advice. It contained information on everything from how to establish an LLC (limited liability company) to questions regarding sales tax permits, trademarks, and copyright basics, among other topics relating to small business basics. I would recommend contacting your particular state small business development center for information specific to your state of residence.

    Now that I had the basic knowledge of where to start, I prioritized my list and then completed my list one step at a time. One thing to remember is that as you move forward, you will continue to re-evaluate your list. You'll update your list by adding new tasks or by deleting tasks that you now know are not needed. I continue to use the goal-setting principle as I grow my business today.

    Another key factor in my success continues to be the confidence and peace I receive by praying for guidance each step of the way. I have no doubt the peace I feel is from the comfort of knowing I am on the right path that is meant for me. As I mentioned above, I have learned to ask, "Am I on the right path? If so, give me the courage to move forward and clear any obstacles from my path. If I am not on the right track, throw obstacles in front of me to make it obvious that I need to head in a different direction."

Projects Versus Goals

    When working with dental teams, I explain that small tasks or "project" lists include anything that can be easily accomplished and doesn't require a lot of steps or involvement of more than one person. Items on this list for a dental office might look something like this:

Project List:

- Sue will purchase a year-at-a-glance calendar by the end of the month.

- Betty will be in charge of writing all team-meeting dates on the calendar as they are scheduled.

- Mary will order name badges for each team member by August 15.

- Elaine will order new scrubs by July 5. All team members will give Elaine their sizes by July 1.

- Sue will begin sending out "We appreciate you" cards to all new patients beginning July 1.

Pay attention to the fact that each task is very specific; it states *who* will do the tasks and by *when*. This is crucial is helping you stay on task and hold yourself accountable for your progress.

A goal would typically require more than one

step and may need more than one person's involvement. Examples of goals you might place on your goal-setting sheet for your dental office would be:

Goals List:

- Incorporate Intraoral cameras into the practice by the end of the year.

- Redesign the schedule to better meet patient needs and streamline to make our days more effective and productive.

- Enhance patient care through more effective communication.

- Design a program to nurture our referrals

- Incorporate more teambuilding programs into the practice

   As you can see, the topics on the list above are more complex in nature and would need to be placed on the goal-setting sheet, broken down into steps, and assigned a name and deadline by each step. Then, these larger goals can be accomplished one step at a time. This process will make accomplishing the goal much more clear and concise and less intimidating.

Start With Where You Are At In Life

Have you ever said to yourself, "If I ever win the lottery I will ____? Or, if I ever have more time I will____?" Why wait? Get your game plan together, and do something each day that will lead you in the right direction.

Pick one thing. What one thing are you going to focus on to make a positive difference in your life? Begin thinking about your short-term and long-term goals. Where do you want to be five years from now? What do you want?

Praying first and planning after may help you stay on course. *Maybe we are planning in one direction, and God's will is in another direction.*

YOUR FIRST TOOL
1. Goal-Setting

You now have learned the basic goal-setting principles. Put this tool in your toolbox, and apply this method to anything you want to accomplish.

Begin a list of the goals you would like to accomplish. Pick one and apply the steps of goal setting using the forms in the back of this book.

_____
_____
_____
_____
_____
_____
_____
_____
_____
_____
_____
_____
_____

Personal Notes

PROBLEM SOLVING

Ok, so you started writing your goals, you outlined your plan and committed to working on the steps you outlined. Then, *BAM,* you run into your first hurdle. You begin questioning your plan; fear and doubt begin to creep in; and you begin listening to your inside voice asking you, "What are you doing?" "What makes you think you can do this?" Meanwhile, if you've shared your frustration with others you may have even heard, "I didn't think you would be able to do that", "I didn't think that would work". Stop! Take a deep breath and remember your ultimate goal. Challenges and problems will arise, however, don't be too quick to change your plan until you have taken the opportunity to focus and think through each of your options.

Let us discuss a second valuable tool that you will find effective if you run across any roadblocks on your path toward accomplishing your goals. There are basic problem-solving skills that, when applied, will help you overcome barriers. The good news is; this process can help to reduce fear, doubt and confusion.

    The following method will help you determine which option will be the best solution for your challenge. You will begin by brainstorming all solutions, then, narrow them down by process of elimination, as you review each solution, one at a time.

The Steps

1. Write down the problem.

2. Write down all possible solutions.

3. Decide on the best solution. Consider the pros and cons of each solution when making this decision.

4. List the steps needed to begin working on the solution. Then put them in order of priority. What needs to be done first?

5. Assign the name of the person responsible by each step.

6. Determine the time/date by when each step is to be completed.

7. Re-evaluate (Is the solution working?).

Helpful Hints
When Using the
Problem-Solving Method:

- Do you need to apply the steps of problem solving to your challenge or is there a simple solution?

- List all the solutions no matter how silly they may seem. As you think of solutions, write them down quickly.

- Begin marking the least favorable solutions off one at a time until you are left with the best solution.

- Begin breaking down the solution into smaller steps.

- Note: Once you have chosen the best solution, the last four steps of the problem-solving method are the same as the steps in goal setting.

A Simple Example

1. <u>Problem:</u> My room is so messy! I'm so busy; it's hard to find time to keep it clean, and I can't find my things when I need them.
2. <u>Solutions:</u> Clean it once a week; spend ten minutes daily cleaning; hire a maid; or re-organize.
3. <u>Best Solution:</u> Re-organize.

*Now apply the remaining steps (four through seven):

Step 4 Detailed Plan	Step 5 Person responsible	Step 6 Deadline	Step 7 Re-evaluate
Buy Containers to separate items	Me	Within 2 weeks	Done
Get rid of things I no longer need	Me	Next weekend	In the process
Put things in their place as I use them	Me	Beginning today	Getting in the habit

This is going great! I am now enjoying my extra space and the time I save by knowing where to find my things!

My Dream of a Website

I wanted to start a website that would help inspire others to follow their dreams. I had an idea of how users could list their products and services while using the site to share their success stories and help encourage others to do the same. It would also serve as a great networking resource for those with common interest. I decided to name it *I Wish I Would Have Thought of That.com*; since most of us have made this statement when we hear about a great idea for something we wish we would have thought of. Feeling a bit overwhelmed and having a limited knowledge of website design and development, I had to decide how to proceed.

My Plan on Paper

Step One: Write down the problem:

- Need and want to set up a website! Where do I start?

Step Two: Brainstorm solutions:

- Hire web designer.
- Find a friend or family member who could do it for me.
- Hire marketing company to build website.
- Learn how to do it myself.

Step Three: Choose best solution by weighing the pros and cons of each solution:

- I chose the last option, as it would allow me to expand my knowledge and learn how to make changes to the site as it grew. It also was the least expensive choice, and given my limited budget, I knew it was a way to get started. I could always hire a web designer at a later date.

Step Four: List the steps needed:

- Find a hosting site.
- Decide on name of website.

- Reserve domain name.

- Design logo.

- Research copyright information.

- Research how to maximize online presence.

Step Five: Assign person responsible:

- My name was by all steps

Step Six: Determine a Deadline:

- Find a hosting site by end of the month.

- Decide on name of website—by end of the week.

- Reserve domain name—by end of the week.

- Design Logo—by 15th of following month.

- Research copyright information beginning today.

- Research how to maximize online presence—

ongoing.

Step Seven: Re-evaluate:

- Find a hosting site. This is working well for the time being and I am learning a lot! I began by contacting friends and family I knew who had more computer knowledge than I did to get more information. Someone told me that they had used hostmysite.com through their work and that their customer service was very good. I contacted them through their website, and they were amazing! I was able to reserve my domain name and sign up for the website service all in one place. If you can follow directions, you can build your own site. They also provided unlimited customer support, twenty-four-seven. Anytime I had a question, I could contact them through their online chat or call by phone. They were always able to answer my questions and walk me through to the next step.

- Decide on name of website—completed.

- Reserve domain name—completed.

- Design logo—completed—however, I had to change my plan and hire a company online. I had spent way too much time and effort trying to do it on my own and was not making any progress.

- Research copyright information—completed.

- Research how to maximize online presence—ongoing.

As the site grows I'll continue to evaluate, if and when, I might need to hire a professional website design company to continue to enhance the site for users.

Following year update and re-evaluation of this website - Whew. How fast technology changes! It become overwhelming trying to keep the website current since this is not my area of expertise. I found it was too time consuming trying to continually learn how to manage this site. I decided to hire a local website designer who designed an amazing website and recommended changing the name to *My Idea Can.* This site was much more user friendly and more professional.

Continued re-evaluation as my goals change: At the recommendation of my website designer, *My Idea Can,* has now been incorporated with my business website, *Judy Risner Consulting.* This made perfect sense, since my business incorporates the same values and principles of *My Idea Can.* This has been a great decision since it reduces time spent managing two websites, while still allowing me to share success stories of others. This was definitely a Win-Win, decision.

Lemonade to Gold

Good Problems Are Still Problems!

By any definition, Amanda was a very successful consultant. Clients reserved time in her schedule months in advance. Her phone rang constantly with potential clients requesting her services. Amanda's staff worked long hours to keep up with the demands of billing, completing client reports, fielding constant inquiries, and preparing myriad documents for her weekly consultations. She was definitely busy, too busy! In light of today's economic climate many folks would welcome such a "busyness problem." So what's the big deal? Why all the drama?

Amanda was stressed to the max. She was working eighteen-hour days, sometimes seven days a week. It was taking a toll on her both mentally and physically. She even felt guilty for having such a problem in this day and time.

Being detail oriented, results driven, conscientious, and mentally sharp are the hallmarks of a great consultant, and Amanda felt herself on the slippery slope of losing her edge. She couldn't afford to let that happen!

She was concerned that her clients would become impatient waiting to get into her schedule and might go elsewhere; that her staff would leave out of frustration; that her stellar business reputation would be tarnished; and most importantly that she, herself, would crash and burn out.

Amanda made the decision to call her friend and colleague, Melissa, for help. Like Amanda, Melissa was a consultant serving the same profession, although in another state. Amanda was confident that Melissa's objectivity and skills in strategic planning would be immensely beneficial in helping her solve her problems. A call was made, a meeting was planned for a couple of weeks later, and flights were booked.

In her office, Amanda sipped coffee waiting for Melissa to arrive. Help was on the horizon! Melissa arrived right on time but without the standard consultant gear consisting of a briefcase and laptop computer. Melissa had only two items; a copy of this book, *Lemonade to Gold: Turning Your Dreams into Reality,* and a pen.

This seemed odd. Amanda had no time to read a book and didn't care for Melissa to read one to her. Amanda had serious problems, and like most people "in pain," she needed quick solutions!

Melissa facilitated and started by turning to the "problem solving" chapter in the book. Melissa and Amanda began to work the steps of identifying the problem, brainstorming possible solutions, weighing the pros and cons of each solution to measure viability, and finally settled on an interim solution and then a longer-term solution.

Both Amanda and Melissa knew that identifying

a problem and coming up with a solution would not get Amanda relief. To breathe life into the solutions, they followed the steps outlined in the chapter on goal setting. Before the morning was over, Amanda had a realistic plan that was written out in steps that were "do-able" even in her current, wacky schedule. Just having a workable plan to reach her goals brought an immediate release of tension, and the fog of helplessness began to dissipate. Regaining a sense of balance in her life could actually become a reality in the near future! Amanda committed to her goals, knowing it would bring the solutions she so desperately needed.

Vicki Sanco, Principal of Journey Management Group; shared this story and is happy to report that a few months later, Amanda was still busy but at a more manageable pace. The interim solution is working. She has enjoyed a few non-working weekends and has begun to shorten her eighteen-hour days to a more reasonable and productive number of hours. In a few months she will begin working the steps toward her long-range goals. It is after all a process…a process that works!

She went on to say, "The simple steps in *Lemonade to Gold: Turning Your Dreams into Reality* can be successfully used once or a hundred times. One person or a group can participate in the exercises; it doesn't matter. The only requirement is to follow the steps with intention. When fully utilized, results will follow time and time again! Just ask Amanda, or the countless others who have reached their goals!"

Epiphanies

Shelly Short, life management coach, will tell you the problem-solving method has been extremely helpful in helping her make decisions and move forward. She wanted to have a business full of passion focused on community and a sustainable work culture.

Teaching has always been a joy for Shelly and sharing what she has learned from her own experiences has allowed her to help others navigate on their path and provide insights that help them have a smoother journey. Shelly once told me, "We are on this planet to help others and provide tools and or skills that make living and working more enjoyable. For me the rough roads have helped me appreciate the smooth roads, and they are both essential for achieving one's aspirations and goals."

She went on to say, "Along the way we have epiphanies, and it is during these moments that we merge what we have learned and experienced into creating something that has purpose and meaning. Defining what I have wanted out of life and asking how I am going to get it have been instrumental in creating the life I am enjoying."

When interviewing Shelly, I asked if she could give me an example of when the problem-solving method was instrumental in helping her make a decision.

Her response was, "It has been a process and putting my options down in writing and working through the pros and cons of each option, has played a key role in helping me stay on task and take steps in the right direction. More importantly I have learned how to be patient and let go of fear. I had to learn again to trust God and believe in the outcome." She went on to say, "A key factor in my success has been a spiritual 'letting go and letting God' and trusting in the process."

For Shelly success is having more time to explore the world with her bike. Knowing she desires balance in work and play, she has sustained her focus by asking herself, "How am I going to get what I want?"

Shelly says one thing she has learned from Zig Zigler is, "We can all get what we want as long as we help enough other people get what they want."

Add to Your Toolbox

You now have two valuable tools in your toolbox to help you on your path.

1. **Goal Setting**
2. **Problem Solving**

Begin a list of challenges or problems you are facing in reaching your goals. Pick one and apply the steps of problem solving using the forms in the back of this book.

_____

_____

_____

_____

_____

_____

_____

_____

_____

_____

_____

_____

Personal Notes

DECISION MAKING

Decisions are a part of life. From the moment we wake up until we go to bed at night, we are making decisions. We make decisions on everything from what to wear, what to have for breakfast, what to buy at the grocery store, to what career path we want to take. Some decisions are simple while others require more thought. Most of our decisions are determined by our wants, needs, and desires, and all decisions have their own benefits and consequences. Weighing those consequences can prove to be a difficult task and can lead a person to prolonging the inevitable: *making the decision.*

Decisions that have life-changing results attached can especially create a lot of anxiety and frustration. When confronted with a tough decision, some of us ask other people their opinions; while others may become obsessed weighing all the options until they are overcome with *analysis paralysis.*

Have you ever had a difficult time making a decision? Do you second-guess whether or not the decision you made is the best decision for you? The following method is a variation of the Franklin T method and can help you bring clarity to the decisions you need to make. Through this method, you can be confident that the decisions you make are the right ones for you.

Moving Forward
Steps to Decision Making Principle

1. What is the decision to be made? Write it down.

2. Make a line down the middle of your paper. On each half of the paper, you will make two columns.

3. Label the columns on each side: Pros and Cons.

4. On one side, list the pros and cons of decision option number one.

5. On the other side, list the pros and cons of decision option number two.

6. Look at your lists.

     Typically, the right answer is staring you in the face. You may notice that one list of pros is much longer than the other. Or, it may be apparent that some of the cons on one list may be more serious in nature, making that decision unacceptable.
The answer is usually obvious.

Is It Time to Buy a Car?

Decision-Making Exercise (Example)

Option #1

Buy New Car

Option #2

Keep old car

Pros	Cons	Pros	Cons
Less repair expense	Car Payment	No Payment	Repair expense
Can get different model			Not reliable
Dependable			Not enough room for family
New car smell			

Now review the lists. The decision may vary depending upon your own situation when making this decision. If finances are not a concern, looks like the new car wins! If the payment would create a financial burden, you might want to opt for keeping the older model for a while longer.

My personal experience using this method has helped me make very big decisions that many times have had a lot of emotions attached. I have found this version of the Franklin T method can help you take the emotion out of your decision and helps you put things in perspective and make sound decisions. You'll also gain confidence in your final choice knowing you have weighed all your options carefully.

Should I Leave My Job?

I had been working for a practice management company for a number of years and loved what I did. My position required me traveling to the client's facility and working with them in their environment. I continued to travel for many years and found my job very rewarding; however, as time went on, I found it more and more difficult to travel on a weekly basis and have time and energy left to take care of myself, spend time with my family, and nurture my spiritual life. I probably would have stayed at this position for many more years had it not begun to take a toll on my balance in life.

After many months of problem solving to find

solutions to help me meet the time requirements of my position I realized there was not a workable solution. I knew at that point I had to make some tough decisions. Should I continue to stay in the corporate environment or should I make a change? You have to remember that I loved what I did, but I wanted it all. I wanted to continue doing what I loved *and* have time to focus on my personal, family, and spiritual life.

And then the emotional side of the decision came in to play, as I had many friends and colleagues within the company I did not want to disappoint. Should I stay so I wouldn't let my colleagues down or should I do what is best for me, and my family? Sounds like an easy decision, but I found this to be one of the most difficult decisions of all. I finally decided to apply the decision-making method to this very difficult decision to gain some insight on which way to proceed.

My Pros and Cons

Stay with current job		Resign from job	
Pros	Cons	Pros	Cons
Steady income	Travel each week	No travel	No income, NO JOB
Love helping clients	Time commitment	Sleep in my own bed at night; be at home more	Will miss working with colleagues
Networking with colleagues	Away from home most weeks/missing family events and special occasions.	More time for self, family, and other interests	No insurance or benefits.
	Stress of travel taking toll on health	Flexible schedule	Will disappoint my mentors & colleagues
	No energy left for family or self or to follow other interests and passions.	Create balance in life spiritually, physically & with family	No concrete plan on what I would do next, will be "in limbo".

After listing the pros and cons of each decision, I then reviewed the lists. Some of the *cons* under my list to leave the company were no guaranteed income, loss of insurance and benefits, and not wanting to disappoint colleagues. For me, they were all major considerations.

Looking at my lists, I weighed the importance of each pro and con in addition to the number of items under each list. There were an equal number of cons under each decision, so the next step was to weigh the importance of each topic. This was still a tough decision because I knew I wanted and needed a balance in life, but if I left, how would I replace my income? After all, I had no plan in place. An important point to make is that throughout this entire process, I prayed about my decision every step of the way. I prayed for wisdom to make good choices and to not allow fear to take me off my course. I wasn't ready to deal with the downside of either decision and continued to pray for wisdom and guidance that I make the decision that was right for me.

Finally, through prayer and weighing the options, the decision was made. I would resign from the company, take a leap of faith, and see where life would lead me. I had such a sense of peace I cannot describe it; only to say that I knew something was waiting for me, and I only had to remain open to opportunities that came my way. For the first time in my life, I had "no plan" and relied on my faith to lead me down the path that was

Lemonade to Gold

meant for me.

Of course, there were days with setbacks and then there were days where I truly felt like a miracle happened when I experienced a major accomplishment. Each day I continue to ask for guidance every step of the way.

Rebuild Slowly

One of my long-time friends and colleagues, Carole Lape, principal and executive business coach and owner of Harrison James Group, shared that she has used the pros and cons technique for many years and has found it to be simply the greatest tool. Especially in 1988, four years into ownership of a museum reproduction business, when an accidental electrical fire claimed their privately owned manufacturing company, to the tune of a half a million-dollar loss in one day. She and her husband were faced with huge choices: *workout* the loan from the bank, file bankruptcy, or rebuild slowly with their own financing. She assured me they did a ton of walking and talking and as a result, they listed many pros and cons. Carole said that listing all the pros and cons of the various scenarios was most effective to lead them to their decision to rebuild slowly. She went on to say it took them only two years, once rebuilt, to regain all of the market share that they had lost as a result. According to Carole, "Seeing all your own thoughts written, instead of spinning around inside your head, is most valuable when you are finally at a decision point. The clarity of the list is remarkable and the pros and cons technique was repeated at every juncture in our recovery. I recommend it highly."

> **Your Toolbox is Growing.**
>
> You now have three valuable tools in your toolbox you can begin to use immediately.
>
> 1. **Goal Setting**
> 2. **Problem Solving**
> 3. **Decision-Making**

Congratulations on reading and learning these skills. Now apply them to your daily life, and track your progress as you travel on your path!

Begin a list of decisions you are facing. Pick one and apply the decision method using the forms in the back of this book.

_____

_____

_____

_____

_____

_____

_____

_____

_____

_____

_____

_____

_____

LIFE-CHANGING RESULTS SHARED BY OTHERS

Kimberly

Beating the Odds Through Strong Faith

I first learned about Kimberly through a mutual acquaintance, and even though we have never met, she agreed to share her story. Her story inspired me because she was able to beat the odds through her strong faith, perseverance, and utilization of basic life skills. Kimberly describes herself as a faithful believer in the Lord and Savior Jesus Christ, and she now celebrates recovery from twenty-three years of substance and alcohol abuse. Today she's seven years clean and sober and lives a life of gratitude and humility full of joy as she fulfills the purpose God has for her life and the lives of her three children. Her recovery has allowed her the true honor and blessing for the first time in her life since childhood to be among the living.

Her journey to recovery and rebirth in Christ began on April 17, 2009, when she was arrested for endeavoring to manufacture methamphetamine. Kimberly was then incarcerated at a correctional facility in Tulsa, Oklahoma, and went on to spend forty days in this facility during what she refers to as a "sanctification period." Instantly, upon booking, she received healing from her addiction and began a walk that would lead her places she had not yet seen in her life. This walk was something she had never before experienced.

Kimberly did not rebel against the structured and disciplined process used by the facility. Each day was the same routine with limited exceptions. Part of the structure included learning how to put what she needed to accomplish into writing. This process helped her quickly realize how this design, would be an asset to her for the remainder of her life. Due to this experience and the principles described in this book, she was able to identify and put into daily use an effective way to accomplish small tasks and goals.

In June of 2009, Kimberly was released on bond with an ankle monitor into a faith-based transitional home. Part of the requirement of this home was to attend a Celebrate Recovery meeting once per week. Celebrate Recovery is a Christ-centered recovery program, and it fit perfectly with where Kimberly was and where she was headed. She witnessed yet another formulated, structured process that helped individuals identify and prioritize areas in their lives where they struggled and had what were referred to as "character defects." Some of these struggles that Kimberly had overcome since being in this program were trauma, co-dependency, enabling, unhealthy relationships, control, inability to trust, and many more. She, of course, did not overcome these all overnight. She has been in this program for her entire recovery and continues to work on what God brings to light inside of her. Once again, by utilizing the programmatic process in which to accomplish her goals and identify her priorities, Kimberly was able to continue on her path of healing.

At the end of the month in June 2009, she was sentenced and was accepted into a prison diversionary program in lieu of ten years in prison. This has continued to be a blessing in Kimberly's life. She spent five hours a day, five days a week in intensive outpatient treatment for one year. All of the goal-setting and problem-solving skills Kimberly had learned to use were reiterated to her in this program and presented and received as "a new way of life." Kimberly stated "I absorbed every ounce of opportunity that was offered me and I continue to this day to utilize and enhance all the wonderful and amazing life skills taught me through these avenues mentioned and provided me by my God who "knows the plans He has for me. Plans to prosper me and not to harm me, plans to give me hope and a future" (Jeremiah 29:11).

She went on to say, "I have learned that in my recovery the most important goal I need to complete daily is to wake up and surrender all to God and His will for my life. As I continue to re-build my life, I carefully approach goals in a structured manner, so as to have continued successful outcomes. I prioritize the things in my life daily that need to be addressed, and I also prioritize short-term and long-term goals. I use effective and viable problem-solving techniques to bring forth the most beneficial and positive outcome in situations. I allow only healthy people who support and encourage my growth to speak into my life. I surround myself with wise, productive, and caring people. I choose to listen more than I speak, and I utilize knowledge and resources for the betterment of all. I was told once to 'do everything with purpose,' and this is a principle by which I live my life, and the tools provided in this book allow me to do just that and much, much more."

When interviewing Kimberly, I asked her why she felt she was successful in her recovery and what key factors could she give us that might be valuable to others going through a similar experience. She responded with the following:

- Leaned strictly on faith.
- Attended every type of class they offered.
- Researched everything she could to learn how to be successful.
- Signed up on every program they offered.
- Had to intentionally be proactive to stay involved.
- Always asked, "How can I get involved?"
- Attended recovery meetings.
- Had to take the pro-active approach to help overcome inhibitions.
- Participated in every ministry.
- Participated in twelve-step programs.
- Attended church services.
- Leaned on the Bible and continued to search for guidance through reading.

- Continued to use the goal-setting and problem-solving, skills she had learned to take a step in the right direction each and every day.

    When I asked Kimberly what one of the most important things she learned throughout her experience was, she said, "Do not allow your circumstances to limit what you yourself can achieve! Number one, regardless what's being told to you, *trust* and believe in what you cannot see. Do not always accept what everyone was saying…don't allow yourself to be forced to believe that something was inevitable. I *didn't* believe that prison was the only option…I refused to accept that there were no other alternatives. I didn't know what would happen but knew prison was not it."

Chris Schutte
An Inventor's Story
The Hot Dog EZ Bun Steamer
and the Steamie

~

    For as long as he could remember Chris Schutte always wanted to be an inventor. Raised by a single mom who saved money on her food budget by freezing everything, he watched her bring frozen buns back to life in her 1960s-style dome steamer. To a small boy, it was like magic. Years later while trying to duplicate the stadium-style hot dogs you get at sporting events, he realized that the secret to a great hot dog was steamed buns. That's when he remembered his mom's bun steamer and thought if she could bring back to life six-month-old frozen buns, there's got to be an easy way to make a fresh-tasting ballpark hot dog at home.

    He said, "I'm already boiling the hot dog in water, why can't I steam the buns at the same time?" That's how The Hot Dog EZ Bun Steamer concept was born. It's a simple little pot insert that works by suspending the hot dog buns in the steam above the boiling hot dogs below. It's quick, easy, and produces perfect stadium-style hot dogs every time.

Napkin Sketch to Working Prototype: Getting Started

  Chris started by placing a cheese grater on top of the pot that hot dogs were boiling in. It didn't quite work; only the bottom of the bun got steamed and the edges got hard from the hot, dry air rising up along the outside edge of the pot. He realized that the buns needed to be down in the pot so a lid could go back on. That's when he discovered that circulation was the key to effective steaming.

  He sketched an idea on a napkin for a grill that hung from the rim of a pot with adjustable hooked handles and headed off to the local hardware store to buy the $30.00 in parts needed to build a prototype in his garage. His initial design produced a fantastic hot dog, but the grill blocked access to the hot dog below, making it awkward to use. That's when it hit him. It was his "ah ha" moment. If he added a cross-shaped opening in the grill, the hot dogs would drop through into the water, and the buns would sit above. When the dogs are cooked, they can be retrieved with a pair of tongs by reaching through the opening in the grill. At that moment in August of 2003, Chris knew he had a million-dollar idea. Chills ran up and down his spine as he thought the concept through for a second and third time. Quickly he built and tested the second prototype with the cross-shaped opening, and he found it worked perfectly. *Okay now what do I do?* Chris thought to himself.

Creating a Business Plan: Setting Goals

Chris spent the next few years working sixty-plus hours a week at his "real job" in sales and marketing for a national consumer electronic retailer. He found himself spending every spare minute reading about the inventing and patenting process. When the economy started to decline, the company he worked for struggled to stay in business. He was desperate to find the time to develop his hot dog bun steaming concept, thinking it was the best way to get off a sinking ship.

Often, when something bad happens to you, it's really a blessing in disguise. In July of 2007, Chris was laid off from his high-paying corporate job and now had all the time he needed to develop his product. He knew he needed a business plan and IP (intellectual property) protection. He turned to friends and family for advice and financial support. That's how he found out about Google patent search and SCORE, a group of retired business executives who volunteer their time to advise entrepreneurs and business owners. Chris's initial plan called for raising $30,000 by selling a 30 percent interest in the concept to friends and family. He then would use that money to secure the patents and trademarks needed to protect the idea, before trying to bring it to market.

That summer he spent most of his time writing a business plan and researching patent attorneys. He decided the most cost-effective way to get started was to use the online legal services provided by a company called LegalZoom.com. Then he backed that up with an experienced patent agent to file the utility patent. After three different patent searches came back with no conflicting pre-existing patents, he started collecting the money from investors and formed the partnership, Innovative Everyday Products LLC.

Manufacturing: Perseverance

Like most inventors, Chris hoped to license his idea to an existing housewares manufacturer and just collect royalties. It's a quick and easy exit strategy but rarely happens in the real world. All of the experts he consulted with said, "If you really want to see your invention in the marketplace, you have to be prepared to manufacture, market, and distribute it yourself." Nevertheless, Chris started soliciting every housewares manufacturer he could find. Most never responded; a few sent rejection letters sometimes months later. It was quickly looking like the experts were right, and the next step was finding a manufacturer.

Using a website called ThomasNet.com, Chris found a US company that manufactured similar wire type products and contacted them about manufacturing a sample production run. Chris knew that his first big opportunity to market his invention would be at the 2008 International Housewares Show in Chicago, which was just a few months away. He would need some finished product in stock to be taken seriously.

Manufacturing a new product, one even as simple as the Hot Dog Ez Bun Steamer, is a much longer process then most people think, and Chris had less than six months until the housewares show. It's at this point when most inventors learn about the one-to-five manufacturing cost-to-retail ratio. If a product costs $1.00 to make, then customers need to be willing to purchase it at retail for $5.00. He thought the most a consumer would pay for his hot dog steamer was $19.95, but realistically it needed to retail for under $9.95, which meant his cost needed to be between $2 and $4. Chris had been waiting for weeks to hear back from the manufacturer with pricing information on the steamer when the first of many devastating setbacks occurred.

The manufacturer came back with a production cost of $19 each, using the one to five rule, he knew customers were not going to pay $95 for his hot dog steamer. To Chris it was like being kicked in the gut. The inventing process is not for the faint of heart; one must pick themselves up after getting knocked down and keep going. This was Chris's first hurdle, so he decided to contact the production manager directly to find out what could be done. The production manager told him the way that the handles attached to the grill was very difficult to produce, and a minor design change could cut the manufacturing cost in half. Chris knew that he could cut the costs in half again with larger production runs. With the new handle attachment design approved, the first manufactured prototype was produced for testing.

  A month later and with only three months remaining before the International Housewares Show, the first manufactured prototype showed up. Opening up the box was like opening the biggest Christmas present under the tree. Compared with the crude prototypes Chris had made in his garage, this unit was beautiful and shiny. Time to start testing. If the Hot Dog Ez Bun Steamer was going to succeed, it needed to work in a wide range of pot styles and sizes. It quickly became clear the handles did not perform well holding the lid in place on a wide range of pot styles, and Chris found himself facing his second hurdle. The only way to have functioning inventory on hand in time for the housewares show was to fly to Houston and drive two hours to personally meet with the production manager at the factory in Shiner, Texas.

  With a suitcase full of different-style pots, Chris boarded a plane for Houston to solve the lid problem. A few hours later he pulled up to the door of this 140-year-old factory and was pleasantly surprised by the good old Texas hospitality that greeted him. Once the production manager understood what the problem was, a solution was only a few hours away, and the next day Chris was on a plane back to Atlanta. Now it was time to get ready for the show.

Market Research and Product Development: Know Your Market

Chris believed he had a marketable idea but still needed some unbiased market research to prove he had a viable product. With a limited budget Chris came up with a creative way to get the needed market research. His idea was to make hot dogs for the on-duty firemen at several local fire stations. While he cooked using The Hot Dog EZ Bun Steamer, his wife asked them market research questions and recorded their answers. They knew they had a winner when one station chief asked for his fourth hot dog.

With a few hundred manufactured units to sell and market research in hand, Chris and his wife headed off to the 2008 International Housewares Show in Chicago. Walking into an exhibition hall larger than a football stadium was overwhelming. Although Chris's wife didn't say anything at the time, she later revealed she feared that they were in way over their heads. Their booth was in an area called the Inventors' Corner and was fertile ground for the news reporters covering the show. As it turns out people like it when you give away free hot dogs, including TV reporters! That night Chris and his wife watched TV as their product was one of only four products featured on the evening news. And why not? After all, Chicago is a hot dog town. For a new inventor trying to promote his product, getting on the evening news was a good start.

Now that Chris was actually selling the Hot Dog Ez Bun Steamer, he started receiving customer feedback. The two things his customers kept saying were "make a bigger unit" and "what else can it steam?" He immediately developed a larger version of the Hot Dog Ez Bun Steamer, and as soon as it was available, his customers started talking about all the other foods they were steaming with it.

Building on the publicity from appearing on the Chicago evening news, Chris was able to land a deal with QVC. In August of 2009, he became a certified QVC guest host and presented the small Hot Dog Ez Bun Steamer and the larger Ez Steam Grill, on national TV. The thrill of appearing on live TV was quickly squashed when the sales results turned out to be far below his minimum expectations. Once again, Chris had to pick himself up off the ground and find a way to keep going. Reviewing the video from the TV appearance and carefully listening to the customers' feedback, Chris started making design changes to take his product to the next level.

The first thing he did was change the opening in the grill to keyhole shaped so it could hold a small sauce dish. This way a person could steam foods and heat up his or her favorite sauces at the same time. Since so many customers were using the grill to steam tortillas, he added a pop-up centerpiece so that tortillas that were larger than the diameter of the pot could be effectively steamed. Watching the video from the QVC appearance, he noticed that lifting the grill out of the pot with oven mitts looked awkward, so he added heat-resistant silicone finger pads to the handles, making it easy to grasp the hot grill. Next he added a clip on the steaming basket so that smaller vegetables could be steamed, and as a bonus feature it could also deep fry. The last thing he did was change the name. The Ez Steam Grill just didn't cut it; the new name he settled on was suggested by his mother, The Steamie. It was simple and said it all.

When Chris combined the Steamie grill, the sauce dish, and the clip on steaming basket into a single three-piece kit, it was an instant hit with everyone he showed it to. Returning to the 2010 International Housewares Show, the Steamie three-piece system was extremely well received. Now there were two distinct products and two different go-to market strategies. The Hot Dog Ez Bun Steamer was best suited to become a clip-strip product hanging next to the hot dog buns in every grocery store in America while the Steamie with its many uses was better suited to be sold and demonstrated on TV.

Marketing: Decision Making

Building on the publicity from appearing on the Chicago evening news and QVC, Chris contacted the PR department for LegalZoom.com and pitched the idea to appear in their next round of TV commercials. The marketing department liked how Chris used several different LegalZoom.com online services to develop his Hot Dog Ez Bun Steamer concept. In November of 2009 LegalZoom.com flew Chris to Hollywood to conduct screen tests for a new TV commercial. The result was one of LegalZoom.com's most effective TV commercials and millions of dollars of free advertising for Chris and his product. Now when he talked to buyers about his product, people listened.

Looking to garner more media attention for his fledgling product, in June of 2010 Chris attended the Inpex Inventor Show in Pittsburgh, where he pitched his new multi-level steaming product, the Steamie, in front of a panel direct response TV experts. By a unanimous decision, the expert panel sent Chris and the Steamie to the New Product Showcase at the Electronic Retailers Association trade show in Las Vegas in September of 2010. At the show Chris was one of forty pre-selected inventors pitching their products to a panel of judges and infomercial experts. When the score sheets were tallied, the Steamie was judged to be the best new product of the show, and Chris was named the 2010

ERA Moxie Award Winner for Inventor of the Year.

The notoriety generated from being named Inventor of the Year led to articles in newspapers from San Francisco to Atlanta. When LegalZoom.com found out that their TV pitchman was selected Inventor of the Year, they asked Chris to record a national radio commercial to capitalize on his success.

Most inventors have very small marketing budgets, and successfully promoting their product is more about self-promotion, free PR, and building on previously noteworthy accomplishments.

Distribution: Overcoming Obstacles

Distribution is the most difficult part, but the most important aspect of the product development process an inventor needs to conquer. Free TV commercials, newspaper articles, and national awards mean nothing if it doesn't translate into sales, and the only way to get sales is through distribution. Before an inventor starts building their distribution they need to have a winning "go to market" strategy. You wouldn't try to sell a pet-grooming product through a lawn care service, would you? That may be an extreme example, but you have to understand where your product fits in the market place and how to best present it.

Nowadays the best place for an

inventor to start selling their product is on eBay and Amazon.com or other similar websites. Setup is easy, and you can quickly learn at which price point your product sells best and how it needs to be shipped. The next step is to set up your own website; Chris set his website up on GoDaddy.com. Again it's pretty quick, but there's enough flexibility to expand your website as you grow. After two years of having his own functioning website, Chris still finds ways to make it perform better and sell more products to the customers that visit his site. The other nice thing about selling online is that you don't have to have retail packaging developed; all you need is just a plain white shipper box, and you're in business. Before an inventor can take his product to the retail market, "high quality" packaging must be developed. "Just good enough" doesn't cut it on store shelves, as Chris would later find out.

The next place Chris took his product was to mail-order catalog companies. Since these companies sell products online or through pictures in a catalog, retail packaging is not needed for this distribution channel either. A plain box and a good product picture is all that is needed. In the case of the Steamie, the multi-function steaming capabilities were lost in a single picture and really needed a video demonstration to be successful.

From the very beginning, Chris believed that The Hot Dog Ez Bun Steamer would be most successful hanging next to the hot dog buns in the bread aisle of every grocery store in America. This is where it's so

Lemonade to Gold

important to know who all the players are in that market space. Chris was able to identify two main players in the grocery store clip strip business. It just so happens that the president of one of the companies walked by their booth in Chicago, and his nametag was spotted by Chris's wife.

    After a quick pitch, a deal was struck to test market the Hot Dog Ez Bun Steamer in a few hundred grocery stores at the end of 2010, matching up exactly with Chris's go-to market strategy. Initial results indicated that the packaging needed to be redesigned and the price point needed to come down. After designing new packaging and lowering the price point, Chris is hoping to re-test his product in the spring of 2012. Hopefully the last hurdle he will have to overcome before the Hot Dog Ez Bun Steamer will make it into the bread aisle of every grocery store in America.

    As for the Steamie, which was selected the best new DRTV product at the 2010 ERA show, Chris created a four-piece version, including the Hot Dog Ez Bun Steamer and presented it on QVC in June of 2011. Although the sales were much better than any of his previous appearances, QVC decided not to reorder, just another bump in the road today's inventors face while trying to get their product to market.

    The important thing to remember is that there is always more than one path that leads to success, as long as you don't give up there always a chance you'll find it. Late in 2012 Chris was able to secure a second grocery store market test with the largest distributor of clip strip products in the country. This time with new packaging and better margin the Hotdog Ez Bun Steamer has its best chance for success it's ever had.

Chris's success in bringing his product to market represents what one can accomplish when you follow your passion, remain committed to your overall goal and stay the course regardless of obstacles you may encounter along the way. His experience clearly shows the importance of designing your plan, following through and then revising as needed when you hit a *bump* in the road.

Adamo's All Natural Pasta Sauce: A Lifelong Dream

~

Janna grew up on her papa Adamo's Italian cooking, especially his recipe for pasta sauce. Her grandfather, Frank Adamo, brought his family's Italian sauce recipe from his home in Sicily via Ellis Island as a young immigrant in 1935. Frank grew up to be a butcher and grocery store owner, as well as a wonderful cook. That same Italian sauce that he ate as a youngster in Sicily has become a favorite of Janna's family and friends who love the robust flavor of fresh garlic, onion, and tomato. There are no artificial ingredients in Papa Adamo's recipe, so naming the sauce was easy!

It has been a lifelong dream of Janna's to share this wonderful taste of Sicily with others. Through the years, family and friends talked about how they would love to produce the sauce to sell in stores for others to enjoy. After much prayer, it seemed the time was right to pursue this long-held dream.

Making a Dream Become Reality

Janna began making her dream become a reality

by setting some initial goals. She identified what she needed to do, wrote it down, and then designed the plan to make it happen one step at a time. She was fortunate to learn about the "basic training program" at Oklahoma State University from the local media. They can help you take your family recipe to the store shelves and can help answer questions such as:

- How much up-front capital will I need?
- What regulations apply to me?
- Who are my target customers?
- How do I get my product to customers?
- When should I expect my business to make money?

The topics covered during the program:

- Planning your business
- Health regulations
- Product and market evaluation
- Labeling and UPC codes
- Patents and trademarks

- Processing and co-packing

- Liabilities and legalities

- Assistance available to entrepreneurs

As a result of the education and assistance she received through OSU, Janna's sauce is now produced by a co-packer, in Tahlequah, Oklahoma. Now that Janna's "Adamo's All-Natural Pasta Sauce" was packaged and ready to go, she had to concentrate on marketing and distribution. I asked Janna what her biggest challenges were as she began marketing her product, and she said, "Limited money and time." Since she does not have any outside investment capital, she markets and delivers her product on a very limited budget. In spite of this, her efforts paid off, and Janna was invited by the national chain Whole Foods Market to be their very first "Made in Oklahoma" product at the Tulsa store!

Janna's Plan

The use of the problem-solving skills helped Janna design a plan to get the word out that her product was packaged and ready for the shelf. Here's an example of her list:

Step 1: List problem:

Need to let people know about my product.

Step 2: Brainstorm solutions

- Go to trade shows.

- Mass e-mails.

- Give away donations of free product.

- Tell friends and family to pass the word.

- Go to local grocery stores.

- Visit wineries.

- Go to small independent businesses that offer food products.

- Join "Made in Oklahoma" products.

- Visit businesses that have items for tourists that visit the state of Oklahoma.

- Research distributors.

- Advertise in local newspaper.

- Get a website.

- Get business cards and hand out.

Step 3: Select the best solutions.

Remember Janna's challenge was that she had limited time and money. These factors would determine which of the above solutions would be best for her at this time.

She began with the following solutions:

- Give away donations.

- Join the "Made in Oklahoma" products.

- Go to a trade show in OKC.

- Visit local stores.

- Get a website.

Now Janna will apply steps four through seven of the problem-solving method to each solution. I'll demonstrate these steps with her first solution listed above: *Give away donations*.

Step 4: List the steps needed to begin working on the solution: *Giving away donations.*

- Make list of who will receive donations.

- Make donations to three stores per week.

- Call first to introduce myself before delivering the donation.

- Visit store 1 week after initial call.

Step 5: Assign the name of the person responsible by each step.

- Janna will be responsible for all steps

Step 6: Determine the time/date by when each step is to be completed.

- Make list of who will receive donations by August 1.

- Begin calling stores by August 15.

- Visit store 1 week after phone call—beginning August 22.

Step 7: Re-evaluate to see how things are going. Do I need to change plan?

- It is going great. Stores are very appreciative for the donations and are spreading the word. Some have placed orders, so this process continues to be time and money well spent.

Taking Charge of Your Destiny

I asked Janna how she continues to move forward with getting the word out about her product, and she said, "I continue to use all three of the methods described in this book while developing and marketing my product. I believe I used the problem-solving method the most in the beginning because I knew my funds were limited, and I could only afford to deliver locally. I have since performed a product demo along with two others done by Whole Foods after the Tulsa store invited me to be their first Made in Oklahoma product. In the future, I plan to continue to market locally until my product can turn a profit. I would then like to market on a larger scale to other states and possibly nationally. The goal-setting method will help me continue to move forward one day at a time as I write down what I need to do next."

Janna said will always be grateful to family and friends for their encouragement and taste testing! She's still waiting for that big break that will allow her the opportunity to ship her product to many other stores around the country! One thing's for sure, Janna will increase the odds of opening the door of opportunity as she takes charge of her destiny by accomplishing her goals one step at a time!

Note: Janna had the pleasure of working with some wonderful people during the development of her product and gives a big thanks to the staff at the FAPC at Oklahoma State University. If you do not live in Oklahoma, you can check with your local universities to see if they offer a similar program.

Tom
Cosmopolitan Insurance and A-Auto Insurance World

~

Most people tell me that realizing their dreams was not an easy road. Many spend years and even decades dreaming about what they want and how they are going to get it. The following story is a perfect example of how one might apply the goal-setting and decision-making principles to realize a dream. These principles in combination with personal dedication, passion about what you're pursuing, a "quitting is not an option" attitude, and lots of prayer clearly demonstrates how you can realize your dreams.

When I asked Tom to share his story, he stated, "I just don't think anything I could come up with would be beneficial to a general audience, and I don't see my story as particularly inspirational. After all, it's not like I had this phenomenal invention or cured cancer." Nonetheless, Tom agreed to write his story and has allowed me to share it with others. I have no doubt that his story will help many others who are going through similar circumstances. Here's Tom's story, as spoken by him.

"After thirteen years in the retail automobile sales industry, I had had enough. I was in finance and leasing and was very successful but never liked anything about it besides the paycheck. I knew I wanted to step out on my own where, sink or swim, I would have control over my destiny. I prayed for a business to invest into and kept coming back to the idea of a fast food franchise.

"I am an analytical thinker and have always believed in asking all the questions imaginable and gathering all the information available before making a decision. I then go to the 'Franklin T' method of reaching a decision. I came up with several categories of things pertinent to the matter and tried to arrange them in order of importance. Income, freedom to do things as I wanted, independence from working for others with whom I seldom agreed, security, stability, and time to be with my family were some of the things I pondered. I then compared the job I had with what I was considering in each category. The car business was lucrative for me but it was sixty to seventy hours a week, little vacation time, and the worst "dog-eat-dog" environment imaginable. I had peace about the decision to get out, so I traded my business suit for an apron.

"We had always wanted to live in Florida where the weather was great and the scuba diving was even better. We took our life savings, moved to West Palm Beach, Florida, and bought a fast-food franchise. With a mild amount of success under my belt, I decided to expand and build a new store near my existing one. I borrowed to build by using the first store as collateral. This began a nightmare that ended about a year later

Lemonade to Gold

with us having to "fire sale" both stores only three days before the bankruptcy was to be filed. Even though the demographics supplied to me from the company looked promising, it turned out that the location was horrible. We lost everything we had, but God was faithful to answer my prayer: I prayed for two months that we would be able to find a buyer and not leave any creditor unpaid, and He came through for us.

"What happened? Was I not listening to God or was I just a terrible businessman? What did I learn from this? After much evaluation, I came to the conclusion that while my intent was good, I had the wrong vehicle and some bad information. I was forty-two, had less than $500 to my name, and had nothing to show for all the time I had saved for my big getaway. I vowed not to go back into the car business and decided to double-down in my quest to make it in business. All of the reasons I had to quit the car business were valid, but I just didn't know what I was getting into. I couldn't afford to make that mistake again. I knew two things: I believed in myself, and I believed that God brought me to Florida for a reason. So now what?

"My Allstate Insurance agent said that the company was hiring agents, but the hiring process was a grueling three-month process followed by months of classes, studying, and licensing. Again, I prayed and asked God to guide me. I heard it said once that all successful people have a risk-taking streak in them. I did the Franklin T again and truly felt that being an Allstate Insurance agent was a much better fit for my skills set. It offered nearly unlimited potential, better suited my morals/ethics, and, if successful, would afford me the balance of work and family that I craved. It would also be my business to run, own, and eventually sell.

"I decided to go for it and was approved in 1997 as the first new agent hired in South Florida since Hurricane Andrew in 1992. I couldn't advertise or hire any staff to help speed the growth since we were broke. I had to pay my own expenses and rent office space, and I started with zero customers. The only way I could even get the final approval from Allstate and open for business was to take out a second mortgage/home equity line of credit at a bank that I didn't even have a checking account at. Convincing a loan officer to take a chance on me may have been the best sales job of my life. That's another time that I felt that this was a God thing.

"I was nervous and excited but still confident that I could succeed on the first day I opened for business. There was no live remote broadcast or marching band to announce my grand opening. I had no money for that. The only sound I heard as I opened the door to the office was the buzzing of the fluorescent lights overhead. I was going to do it the old-fashioned way—talking to anybody who would listen. The checkout lady at the store, the guy at the gas station, and anybody in my area code who dared answer their phone were my new customers. The first day I sat in my new office, I had a phone, phonebook, legal pad, highlighter,

Lemonade to Gold

and a pen. I asked myself, "What have I gotten myself into?" about a million times, but before I got too depressed, I would think about my wife, Becky, and a lot of promises I made to her and myself. At this time, my most inspirational quotation was from the NASA flight support crew during the Apollo 13 mission: 'Failure is not an option.'

"I had a lot of dark days and ups and downs in the first three years, but I stayed the course and worked harder than I had ever worked in my life. I set goals on how many flyers I would pass out a week, how many phone calls I would make, how many mailers I'd send, and most of all, how many policies I would write. I tracked everything—what worked and what didn't, what demographics worked best, and re-invented myself a few times. At the three-year mark, the agency had grown very nicely, and I was finally able to start paying myself. Up to that point we had been living off Becky's nursing salary, the second mortgage on the house, and owed more on credit cards than I would ever admit to a stranger. I had worked very hard, and God had blessed, but I now found myself at a crossroads.

"Since I had gotten into this business at an older age than most, I realized that to get where I wanted to be, I might take one more big risk. The very agent who had spoken to me about becoming an agent wanted to sell out and offered me right of first refusal to buy his and his wife's books of business. This would be a huge undertaking, so I went back to the Franklin T and my prayer knees again. *What if the market conditions or the economy changes? Do I really want to go into $750K debt? Could I get a loan? What if I couldn't make the payments? What if the bank wants a down payment? Handling 1,200 accounts is one thing but what about nearly 4,000?* I analyzed anticipated revenues, calculated cash flows, the higher tax bracket, and a hundred other things. This was a gamble, but I also knew that by adding the two new books of business, I would triple the size of the agency and be on my way to my goal of having an agency large enough that I could sell it, and we could retire on the proceeds.

"Again, I had a peace from God about it and the confidence that I could make it work, so I went for it. Once again, God showed up by helping me secure a business loan with less than 5 percent down. There is a big difference, indeed, between running something yourself and then having to manage others to be successful, but I was able to cross paths with several very bright, hard-working people that helped me immensely. In 2007, I paid off the bank loan, and a few months later I sold the business to another agent at the age of fifty-two. My timing was questioned, but it later turned out that the value of my agency was at its absolute peak at the time of the sale."

What are some things about Tom's story that might be applicable to others reading it?

1. Don't be afraid to dream, but be realistic.

2. Don't be afraid to fail. Know that a failure isn't the end of the world.

3. Before and during the decision process, be honest and objective and become a master of the subject before making the decision. Analyze and evaluate, and then do it again. Get advice from people qualified to give an opinion and help you.

4. Be persistent. Don't give in to discouragement because it can absolutely paralyze you.

5. Have a plan. Have goals. Have the fortitude to stick to plans and goals when the going gets tough.

6. Adapt to changing conditions. Be flexible.

7. Have the courage to back away from a dream if you realize that the enterprise isn't a good fit.

8. Most of all, know God, and seek His guidance.

CHOOSE TO FEEL BETTER MENTALLY AND PHYSICALLY

Many of my goals in life have focused on how I can reduce stress and allow myself to feel better mentally and physically. In turn, being at my best will help ensure I am as effective as I can be in helping others. Of course, some things in our lives are not within our control; however, we can control how we react as unforeseen events occur. There have been studies done by body language experts on how our facial expressions can actually cause physical changes, such as raising our blood pressure. These same studies have found that our facial expressions can influence the emotions we feel!

You're probably thinking, *Sure, if I'm angry, I'll have an angry look on my face,* but what is interesting is this theory is thought to work in reverse. Try it and judge for yourself. Make an angry face and see how you feel. *Smile* and see how you feel. Knowing this sure makes me want to *smile* more!

Throughout this book I have shared some basic life tools that can support you as you continue on the path you have chosen for your life. You have read my experience in using these principles as well as inspirational stories shared by others. Now, if you choose, is the time for you to apply them to your life. The tools you've learned will "help you help yourself." What better day than today to begin on your journey!

Following is a potpourri of tips that have helped me live a happier, more fulfilled life. As you read, select any that you feel would make a difference in your life and write them down. You may want to begin your own list; either way, you will be off to a great start. Next, under each topic, use the goal-setting theory you've learned, and write specifics on how you will incorporate it into your daily, weekly, or monthly routine. Take time on a weekly basis to reflect, and celebrate any successes you experienced. You can use the workbook pages in the back of this book to get you started, or you may want to begin your own personal journal.

Be Thankful, Regardless of the Answer You Receive

~

It's easy to be thankful when something we have asked for has been given to us. Have you ever had the experience that you prayed for something that you thought you really needed only to find out later that *not* getting what you asked for was actually a gift? Did you take the time to give thanks for what you *did not receive?*

A while back, I began buying lottery tickets hoping to win millions of dollars. When I prayed I would explain to God how "If only I could win the lottery," I could help others that were in need through charity work, and how I could spontaneously help strangers that came across my path. Leaving it to God to determine whether or not I would pick the lucky numbers, I would then wait for the results.

I bought a ticket each week. Each time I bought a ticket, I had a feeling of anxiety of some sort. When the numbers were drawn and I learned I was not a winner, part of me, of course, was disappointed that I was not a winner. The other part of me was somewhat relieved. I would often tell my husband, Don, "You know, I don't think I would really want to win millions." My gut instinct told me that it would not bring me the fulfillment that I would get from earning the money through hard work. I knew that winning the lottery was not in my destiny but that something else bigger and better was. I quit buying lottery tickets and am relying on prayer and asking for guidance to show me the direction I am supposed to take. *Be thankful for unanswered prayers as you continue to ask for guidance. Be patient, time will tell…the adventure is not over yet.*

Forgive Yourself

~

There have been many times in my life when I have asked for forgiveness but still felt burdened. I have asked for forgiveness for many things from small to large, that if I had to do over again, I would do differently. One day, while reading the Bible, something that stood out to me was a message about forgiving yourself. I'm sure I learned that somewhere along the way, but somehow it didn't sink in. I feel that I have been good about forgiving others, but what I learned was I also needed to be better about forgiving myself. I have always been my own worst critic, and others have heard me say, "I am much harder on myself than anyone else could ever be." I now know and can have comfort in knowing that once I ask for forgiveness, it is done. I can let it go and focus on the lesson I learned from the situation and how I can use that experience to make me a better person. Forgive yourself. Accept your forgiveness.

Begin a list of things you want to ask for forgiveness and let it go. Then, think about what you learned from the situation and how it has made you a better person today. How can you use this information to help others?

Forgive Others

~

As I learned from reading the Bible; If you want to be forgiven, you must forgive others first. Are there people in your life whom you feel you cannot forgive? How is it affecting you? Is it causing you anxiety? Have you tried to view the situation from the other person's viewpoint?

There have been times when I have been guilty of judging "the person" instead of "the circumstances" that led to the situation between myself and another person. Looking back, I regret the time and energy I spent thinking about how I had been "wronged" and the time I spent telling others about it. I have learned that peace comes with forgiving, and that sometimes this may mean asking God for help. What I can't release and let go of on my own, I ask God to help support me as I work toward forgiving. Asking God to help me understand what I needed to learn from the experience and how I could use this new insight to help others; has been a key component in guiding me further down my personal path.

You might ask yourself:

1. Would it be easier to forgive and move forward?

2. Can I forgive without conditions so that I can feel better physically and emotionally?

3. Can I do this on my own, or do I need to ask for help and support?

Do it for yourself. Make a list of those you need to forgive. Focus on the situation, not the person. Mark them off one at a time as you forgive them.

Make Restitution

~

As I'm accomplishing one of my goals of reading through the entire Bible, I'm reminded of what a great guide it is on how we need to live our lives. One topic that is mentioned numerous times is the importance of making restitution, apologizing, or basically, "owning up to what you've done in the past." While trying to apply what I read to my daily life one day, I sat down to make a list of everyone that I felt I might owe an apology. I could even think of things that happened over thirty years ago in high school that I regretted doing or saying and added them to my list. Then I went down my list and decided whether or not I needed to take action in regard to the names on my list.

I made my decisions based on the fact of whether or not I felt burden in each case or if I would regret not contacting this person if today was my last day. A couple of people I contacted directly, and another one I ran into by coincidence, while another I decided I did not need to contact. In the last case, I realized what I needed to learn from the experience and will remain determined not to repeat the same mistake. What I found interesting was in most cases, the other party and I remember the occasion differently. The other person either did not remember anything about the occasion or it wasn't an issue for them, and they hadn't thought about it since. In one case we had some good laughs, remembered old times, reconnected, and still stay in contact today. So, to my point, only you can decide if you need/want to reach out to apologize to someone.

Begin by asking yourself these questions. Do you want to make restitution to anyone in your life? Can you think of anyone you owe an apology to or someone you mistreated or wronged in some way? Sometimes the other person may not even be aware of how something you said or did affected them in a negative way. Carrying this burden can keep you from experiencing true joy in your life. You can change it today and make a difference.

Lemonade to Gold

Begin by making a list of people to whom you think you may owe an apology. People will have a new respect for you. The reward for you will be in the comfort and relief you will feel when you can then let it go.

I want to apologize for the following situations.

_____

_____

_____

_____

_____

_____

_____

_____

_____

_____

_____

Judging Others

~

Your first impression of a person may be when they are at their worst. Always remember that you are only getting a glimpse of the true person. Give them the benefit of the doubt and look for the good in them. Think of a time when you have not represented yourself well. Maybe you had a really bad day or overreacted to something that happened. Would you want others to judge you by that one instance?

I'll always be on a continued path of learning to be less judgmental. My life experience has proven that many times what I criticize others for, I, myself, am guilty of doing. Think about it. The next time you are judging someone, think about yourself and your own life experiences. Are you guilty of the same thing? Try this exercise. Think about the things that drive you crazy. Then, ask yourself if you have ever done the exact same thing. I did it, and whoa…what a reality check. Let me share a personal example. When eating at a restaurant, some servers will clear your table before you're finished eating. Now, I do understand their goal is to serve as many people as possible, and clearing the table will minimize the time the party stays and munches on leftovers. However, there are times when I want to eat that last bite of bread or nachos and may not speak up when the server retrieves my plate too quickly. While trying to be more aware of judging myself before I judge others, I realized; this is a perfect example of where I am guilty of doing the same thing! My husband and I sit at our snack bar in the evenings, and I usually finish eating before him. So, in my attempt to get the counter cleared and the dishes done as soon as possible, I begin clearing everything I think he should be finished with. If there is any doubt, I would ask him, "Are you finished with the salad? Are you finished with the bread?" Then I stopped in my tracks and realized I was doing the very thing that makes me crazy when I'm in a restaurant. I'm not perfect yet, but I'm happy to report I'm well on my way to getting rid of this bad habit.

Practice What You Preach

Set an example. You will earn credibility among your peers. In my consulting business, I could not in good conscience teach my teams the importance of goal setting, for example, if I did not write my own goals. If you believe in something enough to teach or preach it, you should earn credibility by practicing what you're teaching. The passion that comes through when you're teaching a method you believe in and use, yourself, will be undeniable.

Helping Others

Help someone without expecting anything in return. We all know it's great to be recognized when we go out of our way to do something kind for someone. Most people enjoy being rewarded for their efforts; whether the reward is a few kind words or a tangible reward. I'm finding what's even better is to do something kind for a stranger without telling anyone. I don't necessarily look for opportunities on a daily basis; however, I remain very aware of opportunities as they unfold in front of me.

Not long ago, I was in Wal-Mart and there were several people waiting in line behind an elderly lady who was having trouble locating her money. I was directly behind her and could hear the conversation between the lady and the checkout person. Apparently, the lady was short around $7.00 and was asked to choose an item to put back on the counter. I mentioned to the clerk that I would be happy to pay the difference, but I either was not heard or was ignored. The lady then chose the coffee out of her bag and placed it back on the counter. She was then informed that she now had enough money to purchase the rest of her items. Now anyone who drinks coffee knows that we coffee drinkers *want* to have our coffee.

At risk of embarrassing the lady, I put my arm around her and told her I would really like to buy her coffee, and it would just make my day. She was very appreciative and confessed that she was confused and had possibly left her money in her car. We went on to share a short conversation, and she allowed me to buy her coffee. We were both happy! The lady left, and as I was leaving, a gentleman came up to me who had witnessed the transaction play out, and he said, "I have to tell you, you are an extraordinary woman." I believe kind deeds can be contagious; maybe the gentleman will pay it forward.

Listen

Listen without giving advice. I'm still working on this one! My first response is to help someone solve his/her problem by giving advice. What I have learned to be true is most people just need someone to listen. Recently, I had a business meeting with someone I had never met before, and while driving to the meeting, I began to get a bit nervous. I have learned and taught that when you are at a loss for words, ask questions. So I began our meeting by asking questions, and as it turned out; I spoke probably 5 percent of the time, and the other party spoke 95 percent of the time. After our meeting wrapped up, my colleague said enthusiastically, "I really enjoyed our conversation. I feel like you really understand our needs." This meeting went on to land one of the largest consulting contracts I have signed to date.

Positive Influence

Wake up each morning asking yourself, "What can I do today to have a positive influence on those around me?" And then do it. I have found that some days this is easier to do than on other days. Would you agree? This can be easier than you think. I am finding that if you can't make a positive difference, at least don't share the negative, if it isn't necessary. If you have to share the negative or identify a problem; use the problem-solving skills you have learned in this book, and be part of finding a solution. Many of my clients have shared that one of their biggest day-to-day burdens is they feel they have to solve everyone's problems. Most employers will greatly value employees that take a proactive approach to finding solutions.

Support Strengths

~

Build people up. Support their strengths. Don't focus on their weaknesses. Try thinking of three positive attributes for every negative. Through my years of consulting, I have learned more about the different personality styles. Everyone has their own unique personality style, and each one has its strengths and weaknesses. The challenge is to identify your strengths and how you can use those to be more effective. Equally valuable is learning your weaknesses and how you can build those into strengths. When working with dental teams, we go through the process of learning more about each team member's personality styles and the value their strengths add to the practice as a whole. We also learn about our weaknesses and have many "ah ha" moments. I have heard many times, "That is why you do that! Now I get it." So, when you find yourself focusing on other people's weaknesses, spend at least the same amount of time thinking about their strengths.

Appreciate Those Who Are Different From You

~

They can have much to offer you. We all come from different walks of life. We have a wide variety of cultures, lifestyles, and many different life experiences. I find it very interesting to meet others who are different from me. I know that there is something to be learned from that person. Sometimes we judge others without knowing the life experiences that have shaped the person that we see. Listen to other people's stories that are unique in your eyes. Chances are, they are thinking you are unique. You will find that it opens a whole new world of understanding and will lead to an appreciation of people that are different from you.

Be Spontaneous

Help others in need when a situation presents itself. For example, I was on a business trip and went to the mall to unwind. There was a young man carrying a heavy load of boxes and attempting to get on the escalator. I walked over and helped him carry the boxes.

Lemonade to Gold

He very much appreciated my help and said, "I was wondering how I was going to do this." He appreciated my help, but the reward was mine. It made my day!

    Another time, I was in a busy airport rushing to catch my next flight and noticed an elderly man out of breath and struggling to walk up the next flight of stairs. He was trying reach the top of the stairs while carrying his heavy luggage. Everyone seemed to be in a rush, as I was, as they were walking past this gentleman. I had both hands full carrying luggage, so I did the next best thing and caught an airport attendant who was standing toward the top of the stairs. I asked her if she could either watch my luggage (which was not the best option for either party) or if she would mind helping the gentleman up the stairs. She kindly went to help him, and I rushed on to catch my next flight. This man will never be aware of the small role I played in helping him reach the top of the stairs, but this experience serves as a reminder to me of how many times I have been helped along the way without even realizing it.

"The examples above seems pretty simple, but they can really make a big impact. Here are some other simple ideas with big rewards:"

∼

"Teach to fish." Help people help themselves. Start by teaching them the steps of goal setting and problem solving. I once had a consulting client who was due to re-sign for their next project. When approaching him about re-signing, he stated, "Wow, you have done such a great job teaching us to fish, we can do it on our own." This client had come a long way and was at a place where he felt confident moving forward for the time being. We later reconnected and began working on some new projects.

∼

Think of ways you can bring joy to people through your profession or work and then put them into action.

∼

Do one good deed per day or per week. It may be something as simple as picking up trash off the side of the road. At the end of the year, you will have performed numerous deeds. Others may be inspired by your efforts and do the same thing!

~

Nurture someone in need. For example, take someone to the grocery store, clean their house, prepare a meal, check in on them periodically, or just spend time with them and *listen* to what they have to say.

~

Focus on good habits you want to create, as well as bad habits you need to change.

~

Are you involved in making the world a better place? Start by writing down one thing that you can do, starting tomorrow, and then grow from there.

~

You are not always in charge of the situation you find yourself in, but you are in control of your response.

~

Stay humble. Things can change in an instant.

~

Do some *soul searching* and ask yourself: "What are my true motives behind what it is I am about to do?"

~

Be generous with your time. How can you share your time to make a difference in someone else's life? Brainstorm the possibilities using the goal-setting tool to put your thoughts into action.

~

Spend your time and energy on what you can do better, and reduce time spent thinking about other people's weaknesses.

~

Be aware and recognize when you get answers to your prayers. Write them down and read them as time passes. When you pray for something, you will be amazed at how many of your prayers are being answered that you sometimes take for granted. When you ask for things as simple as finding your car keys to what career path you need to take, always say *thank you* in advance.

~

Pray for wisdom and guidance each day. Just ask God to give you enough wisdom to make the decisions that are right for you.

~

Strive to learn something new every day.

~

Share your knowledge. Identify some of your areas of expertise, and determine how you can use your knowledge to help improve the lives of others.

~

Surround yourself with people who have strengths other than yours. Learn from them.

~

Find a mentor. Find someone you respect that is on the same path that you would like to take for your life. Learn from them.

~

Model those you respect and that are working for the greater good.

~

Never lose your enthusiasm. It is easier to be successful at something if you are excited about doing it.

~

Try to discover what you can do for others without thinking about what they can do for you in return. The rewards will come when you least expect it. I have learned this is a key component in sales. If you focus on how you can help others and don't think about "what's in it for you," you will have positive results.

~

Be thankful for the bad times; there is a lesson to be learned. You will never know if there would have been unforeseen negative consequences if it had happened the way you had planned.

INCREASE HAPPINESS THROUGH THE POWER OF POSITIVE THINKING

The power of positive thinking has strengthened my spiritual life; or, is it that my spiritual life has helped me to be more positive? It's amazing how positive thinking can lower stress and give you a brighter outlook on life. We have all heard that you become what you think about. It's a valid point. Try it. Every time you find yourself thinking negative thoughts, stop and focus on something positive. Continue to do this until you begin to change your habits and your thought patterns. You will find yourself moving toward what you focus on the most.

Your Choice: Create a habit

Begin a list of things you discover make a positive difference in your life and/or the lives of others. Following is a list of suggestions to get you started, or choose your own. Pick one thing and incorporate it into your daily routine; once it becomes habit, then choose a second. Continue adding to your list as move forward.

∼

Never let a day go by without counting your blessings. If you are breathing, you have blessings to count.

∼

Give thanks and appreciation for everything in your life.

∼

Create an atmosphere that is open for communication with your family.

∼

Take time to reflect at the end of the day on the positive things in your life.

~

Turn off news at the beginning and end of each day. Limit the amount of energy you spend on listening to negative news.

~

For the first ten minutes when you get home from work or school focus on something positive.

~

Make certain the conversation is positive. It will set the mood for the evening.

~

When telling about your day, share the positive. Share the negative only when necessary. You will be amazed at how much better you (and those around you) will feel.

~

Be willing to let go of past history.

∼

Develop a new belief system where anything is possible; if you are willing to work hard and pray for guidance. Make your dreams come true!

∼

Ask yourself when shopping, will this make a difference in my life in a positive way…Do I really need this? Would I be better served by putting this money in a savings account? I have learned to ask myself, "Do I need this, or do I want this?"

∼

Think positive about your job situation or begin taking steps to make a change. Work toward creating a positive environment for yourself and others.

∼

Look at what you are doing well, then how can you do it better.

∼

Look at what is not going well. Apply the steps of problem solving that you learned earlier to the situation. Re-evaluate what changes you need to make.

Find ways to make a difference in other people's lives through your work. Think about how you can help them, not how they can help you. The rewards will follow.

Begin your list of things you discover make a positive difference in your life and the lives of others.

_____

_____

_____

_____

_____

_____

_____

_____

_____

_____

_____

_____

Find a Balance between Work, Personal, Family, and Spiritual Needs

~

If you need help in finding a balance, try this exercise. Write down under each of the four topics what you can do in that category to help create the balance you desire. Then, apply the steps of goal setting to each topic. Use the following chart.

Work-Career	Personal goals
Family	Spiritual

Never Let Your Fears Keep You from Accomplishing Your Dreams

~

For many years, a fear of flying caused me a great deal of anxiety for days prior to any time I was scheduled to fly. The challenge was that my job involved travel and flying to clients' offices, sometimes on a weekly basis. I knew I had to address my fears to continue on my career path.

I decided to use the decision-making process mentioned earlier in this book to make a decision on how to proceed. I listed the pros and cons of continuing with my work and flying, and then I listed the pros and cons of changing careers and choosing a path that did not involve travel. Through this method I was able to determine that the benefits of my work outweighed my fear of flying. I began to realize that my work was *part of the plan* for my life, which allowed me to trust that I was on the right path. I prayed that if this is what was meant for me, I would overcome my fear of flying, and I did.

The decision-making method continues to allow me to address my fears head-on and let go of being afraid of what "might" happen. I put my faith in accomplishing my goals and know that I am being guided. I truly feel that there is a plan for me, and that through prayer and hard work, I will continue on the path that is meant for me.

Let It Go

Don't be anxious or worry, present your worries to God and let him handle them for you. Then, let them go.

Your Personal Video

Live your life in a way that you would look forward to seeing it played back before you in front of your family and friends.

My Hope

My hope is that you will gain several insights from this book that you can apply to your daily life that will help you along your chosen path.

Turning Your Dreams into Reality
LEMONADE
to
GOLD

Personal Insights Gained From This Book

Personal Insights Gained From This Book

Things I've Chosen to Apply to My Daily Life

Things I've Chosen to Apply to My Daily Life

GET IT IN WRITING

~

Provided on the following pages are templates for you to use as you utilize the tools you have learned. You may want to begin a journal or workbook of your own and use these as guidelines. Whichever the case, getting your thoughts in writing will help you reach your goals.

~

Goal Setting Exercise

Step 1. Write your goal:

_____

_____

_____

Now apply the remaining steps (2-5)

Step 2. Detailed Plan	Step 3. Person responsible	Step 4. Deadline	Step 5. Re-evaluate

Goal Setting Exercise

Step 1. Write your goal:

_____

_____

_____

Now apply the remaining steps (2-5)

Step 2. Detailed Plan	Step 3. Person responsible	Step 4. Deadline	Step 5. Re-evaluate

Goal Setting Exercise

Step 1. Write your goal:
_____
_____
_____

Now apply the remaining steps (2-5)

Step 2. Detailed Plan	Step 3. Person responsible	Step 4. Deadline	Step 5. Re-evaluate

Goal Setting Exercise

Step 1. Write your goal:

_____

_____

_____

Now apply the remaining steps (2-5)

Step 2. Detailed Plan	Step 3. Person responsible	Step 4. Deadline	Step 5. Re-evaluate

Goal Setting Exercise

Step 1. Write your goal:
_____
_____
_____

Now apply the remaining steps (2-5)

Step 2. Detailed Plan	Step 3. Person responsible	Step 4. Deadline	Step 5. Re-evaluate

Goal Setting Exercise

Step 1. Write your goal:
_____
_____
_____

Now apply the remaining steps (2-5)

Step 2. Detailed Plan	Step 3. Person responsible	Step 4. Deadline	Step 5. Re-evaluate

Goal Setting Exercise

Step 1. Write your goal:
_____
_____
_____

Now apply the remaining steps (2-5)

Step 2. Detailed Plan	Step 3. Person responsible	Step 4. Deadline	Step 5. Re-evaluate

Goal Setting Exercise

Step 1. Write your goal:

_____

_____

_____

Now apply the remaining steps (2-5)

Step 2. Detailed Plan	Step 3. Person responsible	Step 4. Deadline	Step 5. Re-evaluate

Goal Setting Exercise

Step 1. Write your goal:

_____

_____

_____

Now apply the remaining steps (2-5)

Step 2. Detailed Plan	Step 3. Person responsible	Step 4. Deadline	Step 5. Re-evaluate

Lemonade to Gold

Goal Setting Exercise

Step 1. Write your goal:
_____
_____
_____

Now apply the remaining steps (2-5)

Step 2. Detailed Plan	Step 3. Person responsible	Step 4. Deadline	Step 5. Re-evaluate

Goal Setting Exercise

Step 1. Write your goal:
_____
_____
_____

Now apply the remaining steps (2-5)

Step 2. Detailed Plan	Step 3. Person responsible	Step 4. Deadline	Step 5. Re-evaluate

Goal Setting Exercise

Step 1. Write your goal:

_____

_____

_____

Now apply the remaining steps (2-5)

Step 2. Detailed Plan	Step 3. Person responsible	Step 4. Deadline	Step 5. Re-evaluate

Goal Setting Exercise

Step 1. Write your goal:
_____
_____
_____

Now apply the remaining steps (2-5)

Step 2. Detailed Plan	Step 3. Person responsible	Step 4. Deadline	Step 5. Re-evaluate

Goal Setting Exercise

Step 1. Write your goal:

_____

_____

_____

Now apply the remaining steps (2-5)

Step 2. Detailed Plan	Step 3. Person responsible	Step 4. Deadline	Step 5. Re-evaluate

Goal Setting Exercise

Step 1. Write your goal:

_____

_____

_____

Now apply the remaining steps (2-5)

Step 2. Detailed Plan	Step 3. Person responsible	Step 4. Deadline	Step 5. Re-evaluate

Goal Setting Exercise

Step 1. Write your goal:

_____

_____

_____

Now apply the remaining steps (2-5)

Step 2. Detailed Plan	Step 3. Person responsible	Step 4. Deadline	Step 5. Re-evaluate

Goal Setting Exercise

Step 1. Write your goal:

_____
_____

_____

Now apply the remaining steps (2-5)

Step 2. Detailed Plan	Step 3. Person responsible	Step 4. Deadline	Step 5. Re-evaluate

Goal Setting Exercise

Step 1. Write your goal:
_____
_____
_____

Now apply the remaining steps (2-5)

Step 2. Detailed Plan	Step 3. Person responsible	Step 4. Deadline	Step 5. Re-evaluate

Goal Setting Exercise

Step 1. Write your goal:

_____

_____

_____

Now apply the remaining steps (2-5)

Step 2. Detailed Plan	Step 3. Person responsible	Step 4. Deadline	Step 5. Re-evaluate

Goal Setting Exercise

Step 1. Write your goal:

_____

_____

_____

Now apply the remaining steps (2-5)

Step 2. Detailed Plan	Step 3. Person responsible	Step 4. Deadline	Step 5. Re-evaluate

Problem Solving

Step 1: Problem

_____

_____

_____

Step 2: Solutions

_____

_____

_____

_____

_____

_____

_____

Step 3: Best Solution

_____

_____

_____

Lemonade to Gold

Now apply the remaining steps (4-7)

Step 4. Detailed Plan	Step 5. Person responsible	Step 6. Deadline	Step 7. Re-evaluate

Problem Solving

Step 1: Problem
_____
_____
_____

Step 2: Solutions
_____
_____
_____
_____
_____
_____
_____

Step 3: Best Solution
_____
_____
_____

Now apply the remaining steps (4-7)

Step 4. Detailed Plan	Step 5. Person responsible	Step 6. Deadline	Step 7. Re-evaluate

Problem Solving

Step 1: Problem

_____

_____

_____

Step 2: Solutions

_____

_____

_____

_____

_____

_____

_____

Step 3: Best Solution

_____

_____

_____

Now apply the remaining steps (4-7)

Step 4. Detailed Plan	Step 5. Person responsible	Step 6. Deadline	Step 7. Re-evaluate

Problem Solving

Step 1: Problem
_____
_____
_____

Step 2: Solutions
_____
_____
_____
_____
_____
_____
_____
_____

Step 3: Best Solution
_____
_____
_____

Now apply the remaining steps (4-7)

Step 4. Detailed Plan	Step 5. Person responsible	Step 6. Deadline	Step 7. Re-evaluate

Problem Solving

Step 1: Problem
_____
_____
_____

Step 2: Solutions
_____
_____
_____
_____
_____
_____
_____
_____

Step 3: Best Solution
_____
_____
_____

Now apply the remaining steps (4-7)

Step 4. Detailed Plan	Step 5. Person responsible	Step 6. Deadline	Step 7. Re-evaluate

Problem Solving

Step 1: Problem
_____
_____
_____

Step 2: Solutions
_____
_____
_____
_____
_____
_____
_____
_____

Step 3: Best Solution
_____
_____
_____

Now apply the remaining steps (4-7)

Step 4. Detailed Plan	Step 5. Person responsible	Step 6. Deadline	Step 7. Re-evaluate

Problem Solving

Step 1: Problem

_____

_____

_____

Step 2: Solutions

_____

_____

_____

_____

_____

_____

_____

Step 3: Best Solution

_____

_____

_____

Now apply the remaining steps (4-7)

Step 4. Detailed Plan	Step 5. Person responsible	Step 6. Deadline	Step 7. Re-evaluate

Problem Solving

Step 1: Problem

_____

_____

_____

Step 2: Solutions

_____

_____

_____

_____

_____

_____

_____

_____

Step 3: Best Solution

_____

_____

_____

Now apply the remaining steps (4-7)

Step 4. Detailed Plan	Step 5. Person responsible	Step 6. Deadline	Step 7. Re-evaluate

Problem Solving

Step 1: Problem

Step 2: Solutions

Step 3: Best Solution

Now apply the remaining steps (4-7)

Step 4. Detailed Plan	Step 5. Person responsible	Step 6. Deadline	Step 7. Re-evaluate

Problem Solving

Step 1: Problem

_____
_____
_____

Step 2: Solutions

_____
_____
_____
_____
_____
_____
_____
_____

Step 3: Best Solution

_____
_____
_____

Now apply the remaining steps (4-7)

Step 4. Detailed Plan	Step 5. Person responsible	Step 6. Deadline	Step 7. Re-evaluate

Problem Solving

Step 1: Problem
_____
_____
_____

Step 2: Solutions
_____
_____
_____
_____
_____
_____
_____

Step 3: Best Solution
_____
_____
_____

Now apply the remaining steps (4-7)

Step 4. Detailed Plan	Step 5. Person responsible	Step 6. Deadline	Step 7. Re-evaluate

Problem Solving

Step 1: Problem

_____

_____

_____

Step 2: Solutions

_____

_____

_____

_____

_____

_____

_____

Step 3: Best Solution

_____

_____

Now apply the remaining steps (4-7)

Step 4.	Step 5.	Step 6.	Step 7.
Detailed Plan	Person responsible	Deadline	Re-evaluate

Problem Solving

Step 1: Problem
_____
_____
_____

Step 2: Solutions
_____
_____
_____
_____
_____
_____
_____
_____

Step 3: Best Solution
_____
_____
_____

Now apply the remaining steps (4-7)

Step 4. Detailed Plan	Step 5. Person responsible	Step 6. Deadline	Step 7. Re-evaluate

Problem Solving

Step 1: Problem

_____

_____

_____

Step 2: Solutions

_____

_____

_____

_____

_____

_____

_____

Step 3: Best Solution

_____

_____

Now apply the remaining steps (4-7)

Step 4. Detailed Plan	Step 5. Person responsible	Step 6. Deadline	Step 7. Re-evaluate

Problem Solving

Step 1: Problem

_____

_____

_____

Step 2: Solutions

_____

_____

_____

_____

_____

_____

_____

_____

Step 3: Best Solution

_____

_____

_____

Now apply the remaining steps (4-7)

Step 4. Detailed Plan	Step 5. Person responsible	Step 6. Deadline	Step 7. Re-evaluate

Problem Solving

Step 1: Problem

_____
_____
_____

Step 2: Solutions

_____
_____
_____
_____
_____
_____
_____
_____

Step 3: Best Solution

_____
_____
_____

Now apply the remaining steps (4-7)

Step 4. Detailed Plan	Step 5. Person responsible	Step 6. Deadline	Step 7. Re-evaluate

Problem Solving

Step 1: Problem
_____
_____
_____

Step 2: Solutions
_____
_____
_____
_____
_____
_____
_____
_____

Step 3: Best Solution
_____
_____
_____

Now apply the remaining steps (4-7)

Step 4. Detailed Plan	Step 5. Person responsible	Step 6. Deadline	Step 7. Re-evaluate

Problem Solving

Step 1: Problem
_____
_____
_____

Step 2: Solutions
_____
_____
_____
_____
_____
_____
_____
_____

Step 3: Best Solution
_____
_____
_____

Now apply the remaining steps (4-7)

Step 4.	Step 5.	Step 6.	Step 7.
Detailed Plan	Person responsible	Deadline	Re-evaluate

Problem Solving

Step 1: Problem
_____
_____
_____

Step 2: Solutions
_____
_____
_____
_____
_____
_____
_____
_____

Step 3: Best Solution
_____
_____
_____

Now apply the remaining steps (4-7)

Step 4. Detailed Plan	Step 5. Person responsible	Step 6. Deadline	Step 7. Re-evaluate

Problem Solving

Step 1: Problem
_____
_____
_____

Step 2: Solutions
_____
_____
_____
_____
_____
_____
_____

Step 3: Best Solution
_____
_____
_____

Now apply the remaining steps (4-7)

Step 4. Detailed Plan	Step 5. Person responsible	Step 6. Deadline	Step 7. Re-evaluate

Decision-Making Exercise

Option #1   Option #2
_____   _____
_____   _____
_____   _____

Pros	Cons	Pros	Cons

Is your answer obvious? Which list is longer? Are any of the "cons" unacceptable, therefore, making your decision clear?

Decision-Making Exercise

Option #1   Option #2

_____   _____
_____   _____
_____   _____

Pros	Cons	Pros	Cons

Is your answer obvious? Which list is longer? Are any of the "cons" unacceptable, therefore, making your decision clear?

Decision-Making Exercise

Option #1   Option #2

_____   _____

_____   _____

_____   _____

Pros	Cons	Pros	Cons

Is your answer obvious? Which list is longer? Are any of the "cons" unacceptable, therefore, making your decision clear?

Decision-Making Exercise

Option #1   Option #2

Pros	Cons	Pros	Cons

Is your answer obvious? Which list is longer? Are any of the "cons" unacceptable, therefore, making your decision clear?

Decision-Making Exercise

Option #1   Option #2
_____   _____
_____   _____
_____   _____

Pros	Cons	Pros	Cons

Is your answer obvious? Which list is longer? Are any of the "cons" unacceptable, therefore, making your decision clear?

Decision-Making Exercise

Option #1   Option #2
_____   _____
_____   _____
_____   _____

Pros	Cons	Pros	Cons

Is your answer obvious? Which list is longer? Are any of the "cons" unacceptable, therefore, making your decision clear?

Decision-Making Exercise

Option #1   Option #2
_____   _____
_____   _____
_____   _____

Pros	Cons	Pros	Cons

Is your answer obvious? Which list is longer? Are any of the "cons" unacceptable, therefore, making your decision clear?

Decision-Making Exercise

Option #1   Option #2
_____   _____
_____   _____
_____   _____

Pros	Cons	Pros	Cons

Is your answer obvious? Which list is longer? Are any of the "cons" unacceptable, therefore, making your decision clear?

Decision-Making Exercise

Option #1   Option #2
_____   _____
_____   _____
_____   _____

Pros	Cons	Pros	Cons

Is your answer obvious? Which list is longer? Are any of the "cons" unacceptable, therefore, making your decision clear?

Decision-Making Exercise

Option #1   Option #2
_____   _____
_____   _____
_____   _____

Pros	Cons	Pros	Cons

Is your answer obvious? Which list is longer? Are any of the "cons" unacceptable, therefore, making your decision clear?

Decision-Making Exercise

Option #1   Option #2

_____   _____

_____   _____

_____   _____

Pros	Cons	Pros	Cons

Is your answer obvious? Which list is longer? Are any of the "cons" unacceptable, therefore, making your decision clear?

Decision-Making Exercise

Option #1   Option #2
_____   _____
_____   _____
_____   _____

Pros	Cons	Pros	Cons

Is your answer obvious? Which list is longer? Are any of the "cons" unacceptable, therefore, making your decision clear?

Decision-Making Exercise

Option #1   Option #2

_____   _____
_____   _____
_____   _____

Pros	Cons	Pros	Cons

Is your answer obvious? Which list is longer? Are any of the "cons" unacceptable, therefore, making your decision clear?

Decision-Making Exercise

Option #1   Option #2
_____   _____
_____   _____
_____   _____

Pros	Cons	Pros	Cons

Is your answer obvious? Which list is longer? Are any of the "cons" unacceptable, therefore, making your decision clear?

Decision-Making Exercise

Option #1   Option #2
_____   _____
_____   _____
_____   _____

Pros	Cons	Pros	Cons

Is your answer obvious? Which list is longer?
Are any of the "cons" unacceptable, therefore, making your decision clear?

Decision-Making Exercise

Option #1   Option #2

Pros	Cons	Pros	Cons

Is your answer obvious? Which list is longer?
Are any of the "cons" unacceptable, therefore, making your decision clear?

Decision-Making Exercise

Option #1   Option #2
_____   _____
_____   _____
_____   _____

Pros	Cons	Pros	Cons

Is your answer obvious? Which list is longer? Are any of the "cons" unacceptable, therefore, making your decision clear?

Decision-Making Exercise

Option #1   Option #2
_____   _____
_____   _____
_____   _____

Pros	Cons	Pros	Cons

Is your answer obvious? Which list is longer? Are any of the "cons" unacceptable, therefore, making your decision clear?

Decision-Making Exercise

Option #1   Option #2
_____   _____
_____   _____
_____   _____

Pros	Cons	Pros	Cons

Is your answer obvious? Which list is longer? Are any of the "cons" unacceptable, therefore, making your decision clear?

Decision-Making Exercise

Option #1   Option #2
_____   _____
_____   _____
_____   _____

Pros	Cons	Pros	Cons

Is your answer obvious? Which list is longer? Are any of the "cons" unacceptable, therefore, making your decision clear?

Personal Notes

Personal Notes

Personal Notes

Personal Notes

Personal Notes

Personal Notes

ABOUT THE AUTHOR

Judy Risner has worked in the dental industry for over four decades and is now working as an independent consultant to help others realize their true potential and reach their goals. She is owner of Judy Risner Consulting, Inc. and resides with her family in Oklahoma.

Judy's primary focus is centered toward dental practice management, business and clinical coaching. Her expertise includes her experience working as a dental assistant, lab technician, registered dental hygienist and dental consultant for an international dental management company as well as Indian Health Service facilities. Her experience also includes speaking engagements for small and large dental groups and non-profit organizations.

Judy's experience working in a dental office allows her to have a clear understanding of the dynamics and inner workings of a dental practice. Her coaching expertise addresses all aspects of the clinical and business systems related to the dental practice as well as communication skills, team building and leadership training.

She has built an outstanding reputation as a consultant through her unique "hands-on" style of coaching as well as her dedication to working closely with the doctors, clinical team and administration to improve their lives professionally, financially and personally.

SERVICES & PRODUCTS

Comprehensive Coaching
On-site coaching customized for you and your team, working with you in your facility. Your consultations will be organized to meet your specific needs.
Call to discuss how to get started.

Team Meetings
Are you currently having team meetings? Let us join you to discuss any topic of your choice and design a plan for immediate implementation.

Study Clubs
Do you need new topics for your local study club? This is your opportunity to share any challenges and work with us to find solutions.

Dental Meetings
Need a speaker for your local dental meeting? We offer speakers on most topics in the dental

arena, including health and wellness.

Telephone Support
Need someone to listen to your challenges and offer tools to help you find solutions? We're here to help and support you as we brainstorm solutions.

CONTACT INFORMATION

Email: judy@judyrisner.com

Mailing Address:
P.O. Box 425,
Davis, OK 73030

TESTIMONIALS

"I feel Ms. Risner has the unique ability to teach without preaching and motivate while teaching. She can lead you to the place where you make the biggest impact on your patient's health and makes it enjoyable to get there." DDS, MD

"If your Dental Practice gross income is under 5 million per year, and you want to hit that target before you retire, your best investment is Judy Risner. She'll create loyalty, peace, harmony and drive in your employees; streamline and improve your procedures, teach your hygienists and doctors how to make patients love them, show you how to improve profitability, and so much more....all you need to do is believe in yourself and make sure you do absolutely everything she tells you to. You will be so happy you met her, and so happy you followed her advice. She is a miracle worker. I have worked with scores of consultants and thousands of practices on their technology plans and their business plans. When Judy was involved, the practices absolutely sparkled with excitement, growth, and innovation." D. Redwine; Network Management Systems

Architect at CompuCom

"I believe what worked so well was her ability to really communicate with our staff while effectively introducing real world concepts of communication and team building all while generating a wonderful sense of enthusiasm and loyalty in our staff! At the end of our very productive session with Judy, the one question everyone asked was 'when is Judy coming back?' "- DDS, MA.

"Judy performed her job with the utmost professionalism and insight. She was often able to effectively draw on her broad background of experience in the field of dentistry with first hand knowledge. She is much attuned to the various inter-working dynamics." DDS, OK.

"She has excellent communication skills and a thorough knowledge of her subject matter. She has the ability to be firm and yet non-intimidating while exhibiting care and compassion."   DDS, OK.

"With Judy's help we were able to improve our communication with patients and each other. Our production increased during her time with us! All in all it was a joy and a pleasure to work with Judy." DDS, LA.

CONTRIBUTORS

Vicki C. Sanco. Principal Journey Management Group, LLC. Consulting, Coaching, Practice Development Solutions for the Dental Profession.
www.journeymanagementgroup.com

Shelly Short, RDH, MS, PhD, Life Management Coach and Co-Creator Zum Group – A (To Your Health) coaching company that incorporates a Wellness Approach to Business and Life Management.
www.zumgroup.us

Carole L. Lape, BA, CEC, Principal & Executive Business Coach, Harrison James Group - "a company dedicated to open communication and customized systems for small business owners, teams and leaders".
www.harrisonjamesgroup.com

Kimberly Cummings, Executive Assistant, Mental Health Association in Tulsa. www.mhat.org President, Circle of Life Board, graduate community aftercare program. Vice-President, Just the Beginning Inc. justthebeginninginc.org
Training Coach, Celebrate Recovery Greenwood Christian Center.

Chris Schutte, Inventor of the Hotdog Ez Bun Steamer and Steamie; Chris is the Winner of the 2010 ERA Moxie Award for "Inventor of the Year". Innovative Everyday Products LLC (678) 472 -5016 www.hotdogezbunsteamer.com and http://blog.aninventorsjourney.com/

Janna M. Adamo, CEO, Adamo's All Natural, LLC. Adamo's All Natural Pasta Sauce. www.adamosallnatural.com, email jadamo2@cox.net , (918) 638-5744

Tom Brown, Owner of Cosmopolitan Insurance and A-Auto Insurance World in W. Palm Beach Florida email thomasbrown1954@gmail.com

"I welcome any comments, suggestions, or testimonials you would like to share. I would love to hear from you and read your success stories. If you would like to share your story email me at judy@judyrisner.com."

"Thank you for reading this book. I am truly honored. If you have benefited from the time you spent, please tell others. The referral of your family and friends would be my highest compliment."

Judy

If you would like to share this book with others;
Order more copies
@
www.amazon.com